# RICK BATEMAN
## BRILLIANCE FLAWED

*A True Life Novel of the Man
Behind the Myth*

**Jude Ann Burk**

**Parker House Publishing**
ParkerHouseBooks.com

Published by Parker House Publishing
ISBN: 978-0692511343

Cover design: Laura Pichard-Murphy, Paisley Design, Tallahassee, Florida
Rick Bateman back cover portrait - Rick Bateman archives
Jude Ann Burk back cover portrait - David A. Pasquarelli

Inside photo credits:

Rick Bateman and Steve Bateman as toddlers - Freddie Bateman personal collection.
Rick Bateman high school portrait - Freddie Bateman personal collection.
Rick Bateman and Laura Lane Heidrich college sweethearts - Laura Lane Heidrich personal collection.
Rick Bateman, Freddie Bateman, Mary Lynn Bateman, Todd Bateman, Steve Bateman, Bert Crosson group photo – Freddie Bateman personal collection.
Rick Bateman and Clay Campbell - Jude Ann Burk personal collection.
Rick Bateman with toddler daughters at Woodbine - Freddie Bateman personal collection.
Rick Bateman and Columbian boy with bird - on loan from R. Lee Barrett personal collection.
Rick Bateman gator hunting at night – Rick Bateman archives.
Jude Burk and Debbie Dantin kissing Rick's photo at Finnegan's – Debbie Dantin personal collection.
Rick Bateman, President Bill Clinton, Bill Pfeiffer - Bill Pfeiffer personal collection.

This book is intended to provide information and entertainment. The content is a collection of recorded personal interviews conducted with the author, information obtained through archives and public records, and the personal recollections of the author. The information and opinions expressed are the sole expressions and opinions of the author and contributors listed herein.

# Acknowledgements

The following individuals generously shared their stories and resources, without which this book would not have been possible:

Benjamin Webster
Bryan Desloge
Charles M. Ward, II
Christina Delk
Damien Prosser
Dana Morris Brooks
David A. Pasquarelli
David Oliver
Doug Dickinson
Freddie Bateman
Gary Yordon
Gregory M. Luce
J. Lee Vause
John Morgan
Julie Connell-Smith
Kari Rowe
Keith Dantin

Kevin M. McCarty
Laura Lane Heidrich
Lynn Szymoniak
Mary Lynn Bateman
Matthew R. Willard
N. Todd Bateman
Regan Jager
Rex Shiver, Sr.
R. Lee Barrett
Ronald Brafford
Roy Bedard
Ruben Rowe, III
Sonya K. Daws
Steven Leoni
Vincent S. Long
William "Bill" Proctor

*For Rick...*
*I promised you I would write your story.*

# Contents

# Prologue

I could feel his presence before I saw him. His large, but compact frame was sitting in a crouched position in one of the winged back Louis XV chairs in the law office reception area. His shaved head, topped with a tattoo of a dagger and an eye dripping blood, was looking down at the oriental carpet, while his left leg bounced up and down in a nervous twitch. He had no neck that I could discern and the white tee shirt he was wearing strained under the stress of covering his massive chest as it heaved back and forth like a bull ready for charge. *Great!* I thought as I walked toward him, *a gang banger to start my day! But, everyone deserves legal representation*, I mused, *so let's see what Legal Aid has sent our way this time.* "Mr. Smith?" I asked. He looked up and said in a voice that startled me with its smallness, "Yeah, he me." I reached out to shake his hand as he stood up, but his right hand was occupied with holding up his too big jeans (a gang dress code to imitate an inmate whose belt has been taken away by authorities). His left hand was clutching a piece of paper that he poked at me. "Let's go into the conference room and get the paperwork out of the way before Mr. Bateman arrives," I suggested.

As I turned to walk toward the conference room, I was surprised by another larger man standing behind me. I gasped loudly, "Who are you?!" "He my driver," Smith answered for him. "Oh, I didn't see him when I came in. Will he be joining us during our meeting?" "Naw, he just sit outchere and wait 'til we done." At that, the driver sat down and folded his arms across his chest, causing his shirt to pull up from his waist and reveal the handle of what I guessed was a very large knife. At this point, I decided to leave open the double pocket door separating the reception area and the conference room. I wanted to keep an eye on the knife wielding driver and the front door in case other gang members decided to hook up with their brothers.

I pointed to a chair at the end of the long mahogany table for Smith to sit in. I pulled one to the left of his, near the door, where I could make my retreat as soon as Rick showed up. *Why the hell was Legal Aid sending us a criminal case when they know damn well we're a civil law firm!* I wondered angrily as I tried to control my growing irritation with Rick's habitual tardiness. Here I was, by myself in this large suite of offices an hour before anyone else would arrive, to gather preliminary information from Mr. Smith so the pro bono time wouldn't interfere with the rest of the day's busy schedule of paying clients. As I opened my file and began to review the wrinkled piece of paper Smith had brought with him, I was imagining several escape scenarios I could use if he and his "driver" decided they'd had enough of me. I was mentally scanning all the places in the building where Rick had guns hidden, all fully loaded, and how fast I could possibly run in heels with my arthritic legs. Smith interrupted my thoughts of flight with a question: "You gonna fix it with that bitch?" A quick glance at the paper on the table gave me the clue I needed to respond. "It appears that you have been sued for non-payment of child support," I explained as I pointed to the court summons. "Ms. Lamika

Jackson is the Plaintiff on the summons. I assume she is the mother of your child?" "She my baby mama and the bitch know I ain't got no money to give her for nothin'! You can tell her that...right?" *Damn you, Rick Bateman, where are you?!* I was screaming inside. "Mr. Smith, let's just get some paperwork out of the way and I'm sure Mr. Bateman will be able to answer all your questions as soon as he arrives, which should be any minute now," I said hopefully. "Please give me just another couple of seconds to review your file so we can get a handle on what needs to be done for you." I was trying to buy as much time as possible, knowing full well that Rick probably found something else to occupy his morning, most likely a woman, and I would have to keep this thug entertained longer than I had patience to do so.

The date on the summons caught my eye. "Mr. Smith, this summons calls for you to be in court two days ago!" I said with an urgency I hoped would send him running out the door. "I's busy. You call the judge's peoples and tell them that." "No, Mr. Smith. You can't ignore a summons like this. The court can find you in contempt and have you arrested. What were you doing that caused you to miss your court date?" I asked, surprising myself at my sudden interest. "I's in jail," he said nonchalantly. "What?!" I heard myself say much too loudly and causing the driver to look up from his post on alert. "What do you mean you were in jail two days ago? What caused you to be there?" "I cut my baby mama, but she say later that she sorry she called the cops and told them she changed her mind." "Wait a minute," I pushed further, "Ms. Jackson is summoning you to court for back child support and knew you were in jail for cutting her?" "Naw, that Sherree, my other baby mama I cut."

3

My head was pounding with all manner of questions, insults, and outrage. I decided this meeting was officially over. "Mr. Smith. I'm very sorry. Legal Aid has sent you to a law firm that does not handle family law or criminal law. I will call them as soon as you leave and tell them to get you an attorney who can help you on all of your support and contempt of court issues. I will discuss all of this with Mr. Bateman when he arrives and if there's anything else he thinks we can do for you, he can discuss that with the attorney appointed to you." I quickly stood up before he could say anything that would cause the driver to get an itchy finger and reach for his knife. Smith pushed himself away from the table, grabbed his pants and turned to walk out without saying anything. I could no longer restrain my pent up anger with Legal Aid, Rick, and society in general. "Well, anyone can see that you don't have any money to pay your child support since you can't even afford a belt to hold up your pants!" I spitted out with a forced smile as the two gangstas shuffled out the front door.

Two hours later, Rick came breezing in, walked right by my office, and flopped down behind his desk across the hall. I was on his heels. "Good morning, Mr. Bateman!" I said sarcastically. I called Rick "Mr. Bateman" when I wanted to formalize whatever I was about to say, mostly in front of clients, but when it was just the two of us it served as a signal for him to know I was either getting ready to talk about something financial or otherwise unpleasant. "Good morning," he said suspiciously as he looked up from his cell phone that too often occupied his attention. "I want to share with you the lovely meeting I just had with one of the pro bono clients Legal Aid sent over to us. You remember pro bono cases that you agreed to take, don't you? Well, Mr. Smith was one of them and he was here bright and early this morning as we all agreed to – 7:30 a.m." No reaction from Rick. I apprised him of the whole episode, including my parting shot about the belt. "God damn, Jude! Did you really say that?!" he cackled. His laughter was getting on my last nerve and I released a venomous litany of abuses I'd suffered at his hand. "Yes! I really said it! Somebody had to say or do something because you certainly weren't here to do so! This is getting ridiculous! You agree to meetings and don't show up, so I have to tap dance and keep clients, even gang bangers, believing that their cases really matter to you. The banks call and want to know when we might be making a deposit to cover the checks that are clearing without funds in the account, because you either can't or won't ask clients for payments. So I have to play bill collector and track them down! I'm writing checks from my own account to cover payroll! Interns are writing crap complaints that I have to proof and correct because you aren't here to share your legal brilliance with them!" Before I could finish my tirade (and I was really getting to some deep down resentment that I'd been storing inside for years), Rick stood up and walked over to me with a look on his face that was a mix of surprise and sadness. "Well, what can I say, Jude? You're my everything!"

And so it was that I navigated the wild and crazy ride of managing the business and personal life of Rick Bateman. He called me his "office wife," and in a sense I guess that's what I was. I loved him and hated him, sometimes simultaneously. I suspect he felt the same toward me. We trusted each other and never made promises that we didn't keep. This book is the fulfillment of my last promise to Rick.

One day in the midst of the media circus surrounding the "Girls Gone Wild" litigation (during which Rick met his dysfunctional match in his client, Joe Francis), he came into my office and said in that loud, gravely voice that could wake the dead, "Jude, we either need to do a reality series about me or you need to write my story!" "Well, Mr. Bateman," I said dryly. "If we end up doing a reality series, you'll have to pay for my facelift before the cameras start rolling. Or, if the Cosmic Joker has his way and you die before me, I'll write your story. But, it will be the truth - good, bad, and ugly - or it won't be told." "Deal!" he laughed and shook my hand. Deal indeed. At eight years his senior, I never thought I would outlive him, even when he seemed bent on his own destruction with his toxic lifestyle. His constitution was such a strong force that he always had a way of bouncing back from anything that bothered him. But, his karma was played out three years after we made our deal in his sudden death at the age of fifty-five.

I originally intended to write a compilation of stories about Rick that dozens of friends and family members told me they would share. Time and circumstances change things, and many of the people who I reached out to and were the closest to Rick have gone silent with their memories. Therefore, this book is my version of Rick's life based on my own personal recollections. They are complemented by anecdotal references gleaned from interviews, public records, and shared confidences. Some names have been changed to protect the privacy of those who prefer it, and some of the legal cases referenced are enhanced representations of real ones that Rick litigated. It is not my intention to analyze or judge why and how Rick behaved. His life was too complex and his motives unexpressed. Nevertheless, it is written to the best of my ability to reflect those events and relationships he experienced, and to deliver his story with unconditional love.

# Chapter 1

## *Who was Rick Bateman?*

The life of Rick Bateman was a many splendored one. Like a brilliantly cut diamond, it sparkled and cast a fine light that embodied all the colors of the rainbow. And, like the fissures and carbon deposits that flaw a diamond, the brilliance of his life was marred by an inherited negative energy for which he could find no resolution.

That he was a supremely talented litigator was undisputed by friends and enemies alike. His ability to envision the complete battle plan for a complex legal case, and know exactly when and how to strike his attack, made him the warrior everyone wanted on their side. Much of what he knew came from the excellent education he received at two elite institutions. But the lion's share of his cunning and intuitive nature were notched into his soul as his birthright, culled from generations of macho, high performance Bateman men. It's been said that we all suffer from our origins, and the emotions of previous generations constantly surround us.[1] Rick came from a long line of super males who excelled in the art of the deal, but when it came to personal commitment, couldn't plant their feet for long in any one place and whose wounds were largely self inflicted.

_____

[1] Adyashanti, "Falling Into Grace"

Frederick Leo "Rick" Bateman, Jr. was born to Freddie and Peggy Bateman on March 11, 1957, in Camilla, Georgia, the eldest of three boys and one girl. He always considered himself a red clay Georgia boy and was proud to be from a working farm family. His heritage was English and American Creek Indian. Rick's paternal grandfather, Leo, worked for St. Joe Paper in Bristol, Florida. He was the only one who the company trusted to walk a piece of land, decide how much timber it would yield, and buy it on their behalf. "He knew instinctively how much money you could get out of a piece of land," Freddie shared. So, he decided to start amassing land for himself and passing it on to his children and grandchildren as stakes to begin their lives. Freddie would spend his life tending to the estate that his father had compiled and never had to worry about finding employment outside the family compound. "Daddy was spoiled, always worked for his father and never really had to work that hard for anything," declared one of his sons.

Physically, Rick was an imposing figure. Six feet, four inches tall, he boasted an athletic, yet supple physique. His head was crowned with thick, coal black hair. His face was punctuated with penetrating brown eyes framed with unkempt fringes of black brows that had never yielded to a barber's scissor. His inside voice was the same as his outside voice and could penetrate the sound barrier of a two-story, 3,500 square foot home without any strain to his vocal chords. He had a quixotic demeanor that was tempered by an inexhaustible search for knowledge. He had to challenge everything to assure himself that what was being put forward as fact was indeed so and not just generally accepted belief. Maintaining his attention was like trying to hold Jello on a wall. Wearing socks was anathema to him.

Rick loved and feared his father. It was this psychological conflict that was responsible for the two radically different personas that he presented to the world. One was a mean, crass and vengeful man, and the other was a benevolent, sociable comrade, whose generosity and goodwill to all earned him devotion and love from legions of men and women alike. When he would finalize an especially complicated land deal and then call his father to tell him about it, I could hear Rick's voice change as Freddie picked up the phone. The little boy who would do anything to win his father's admiration had bobbed up from inside him to take over the call. "Rick was the one you could tell was the apple of his father's eye," his friend and neighbor, Charlie, said. "It was like my dad. He died at ninety-two, and up until his death I feared him, but I sure loved him!  He'd ask me to jump, and I'd say how high? That's the way I could tell Rick was with his dad."

Freddie bred competition in his boys and would gather them up as toddlers, put them in a circle and command them to fight with one another until only one was left standing. This scene played out multiple times, all the way through their teens. "Daddy wanted to be sure we were tough enough to take on anybody at anytime," Rick's brother Todd related. "There's a lot of sons of bitches out there and you need to be the biggest and baddest one if you're going to survive this man's world," Freddie would warn the boys.

Ms. Peggy had her hands full with her energetic boys, and lots of bloody noses and broken bones were evidence to that fact. They were the Three Musketeers, who would compete with and assault one another, but would unite to visit hell upon anyone outside the family circle who said a harsh word or picked a fight with one of them. Rick was the ring leader for most of their daredevil antics, two of which involved a set of monkey bars that Freddie had installed in the backyard for the boys to swing from and strengthen their upper bodies. Todd shared these stories from the time that Rick was around six, Steve five, and Todd three:

*When we were young we had monkey bars. I was too little to really swing from them, so Steve and Rick got me on a tricycle and were going to push me through a small opening on the bottom between the bars. They gave me a real hard heave ho and sent me forward faster than my little feet could pedal. My head grazed a screw sticking out on one of the lower pipes and I bled all over the place. I cried, they cried, Mama cried, and Daddy laughed.*

*Another time we got in trouble with those dang monkey bars was when Rick had the idea to push them over to a big chinaberry tree so we could climb up on top and then we could swing from an electrical wire that hung from the house. The wire was connected to the well that provided our water. Steve was the first to try it and as soon as he grabbed the wire he got knocked right off the monkey bars. I went next and also got knocked off as soon as I grabbed the electrical wire. Then, Rick grabbed it and don't you know the same thing happened to him! We were all crying and hurt everywhere. We didn't know the electricity had done it. We all got beat real bad for that.*

Freddie transmitted his prowess on the football field to his eldest son. The patriarch had been a star quarterback at Mitchell County High School. His "take no prisoners" style of play brought championships to the school and secured him the prestige of being the first player of any sport to be installed in the school's athletic Hall of Fame. Unlike his father, however, Rick's battles for yardage on the football field won him a different kind of recognition. Rick played center and defensive linebacker positions. He'd target the opposing team's best player and purposefully make moves to trigger retaliatory actions, resulting in on field brawls between players, coaches, and the home school's principal. "He was a real ruffian," according to one school official, and was kicked out of several games. The local media dubbed him, "The Thrilla from Camilla."

Rick received scholastic and athletic scholarships to attend Davidson College, considered to be the "Harvard of the South", in Davidson, North Carolina, where he received his Bachelor of Arts (B.A.) degree. He went on to the University of Florida in Gainesville, Florida, at which he earned his Juris Doctorate in Law (J.D.), and served as a Teaching Fellow. He was a member of Kappa Alpha fraternity where he made lifelong friends, who in the decades to follow would both admire him and worry for him.

Throughout his college career, Rick was known as a ladies' man and could balance dates with three different co-eds on the same night without any of them knowing about the other. In fact, it would be his lifelong "modus operandi" to give each of his lovers the impression that she was "the only one" in his life. His charm and wit allowed the deceit.

> *He had more girls than you could imagine! When he spoke to someone, they thought they were the only one. He meant it when he said it until he met the next one. He had the unique ability to fool himself. I don't think he had any personal insight on who he was and what would make him happy. Drinking, screwing, and making money was what he thought would make him happy.*

One special woman stood out from the others and would remain part of Rick's life as long as he lived. He told me about her, referring to her as his soul mate, and said he regretted not fighting harder for her when he was younger. Her father disapproved of Rick, cautioning his daughter that he couldn't be trusted.

> *I met Rick in 1977, when I was attending Queens College, a girls' school about thirty minutes away in Charlotte, North Carolina, and Rick was at Davidson. Charlotte was thirty minutes away, so there was always a lot of active traffic between the two schools! He was my first date, a blind date that a sorority sister set up. I was eighteen and he was twenty. We dated from that point on for many years until I*

*met my husband. There were many proposals, but Rick was a character. Rick was bigger than the room most of the time. I'm a big personality myself, but when we were together there were fireworks. We were both strong willed and opinionated which got in the way sometimes, but the love was always there.*

Freddie had strayed many times during his marriage to Peggy. Despite her resolve to keep the family together, one woman too many resulted in her filing for divorce. Not long after that relationship ended, Freddie married for a second time. It turned out to be a loveless union and lasted just eight years. During that time, however, he once again ventured outside of his marital boundaries and began an affair with the wife of a Camilla neighbor. The liaison resulted in a pregnancy, with the patrimonial tie to the boy remaining a secret for thirteen years. When the couple could no longer bear living apart and having to settle for illicit trysts, Mary Lynn filed for divorce from her husband and married the love of her life. During the court proceedings to end the marriage, it was finally revealed that the child named Bert Crosson was actually the son of Freddie Bateman.

After graduating from law school, Rick had moved to Orlando and tended bar at Rosie O'Grady's. He stayed with his mother and stepfather until landing his first law firm job in insurance defense. It was around this time that Rick discovered he had a third brother. The news finally made its way via the grapevine to Rick. So, he jumped in his car and drove to Camilla for a first hand look. He told me the story one day after he finished a phone conversation with Mary

Lynn about plans for the upcoming Thanksgiving holiday. "Yeah, I took one look at Bert and knew he was one of us," Rick said. From the moment they met, Rick loved and acknowledged Bert as his baby brother. One of the more touching moments at Rick's graveside service was when Bert told the story of that first meeting and how much Rick had always been there when he needed advice, financial assistance, and a brother's love.

Rick married for the first time on October 24, 1987, to Donna Maggard in Orlando. Rick met Donna when she was a court reporter in one of the courtrooms in which he appeared for cases. Lee, his college roommate at the University of Florida and future trustee of the Bateman Daughters Trust, shared the event:

> *He saw her and he was smitten. She had that New Jersey girl personality. She was smart and quick and he loved that. But, Rick had a wandering eye so they broke up for a while. I'd never seen Rick cry before then. He was devastated and stayed in his room drinking vodka for two days when he heard she'd gone out with someone else. He told me he had to get her back. I said, "Rick, don't do that to her - don't get her back and screw with her head." "No," he answered, "I'm going to be a good boyfriend." He did win her back and they got married.*

The couple was blessed with twin daughters, Kathryn Madison "Madi" Bateman and Callie Harden Bateman, on

September 25, 1990. To say they were adorable would be a gross understatement. Rick kept one particular photo of them, when they were probably one-year-old, on his credenza. It made me swoon every time I saw it. Bare feet, dressed in white baby gowns, each holding on to the sides of a white Adirondack lawn chair, and both giving wide "gummy" grins. Rick cherished his daughters and referred to them as his "treasures." They would be the only women in his life to whom he remained loyal and steadfast in his love.

By the time the girls were born, Rick's social life was in full swing as a result of his professional success. He and Donna kept a cadre of babysitters on standby for a growing calendar of events that were "must attends." One of the sitters shared her experience tending to the Bateman daughters:

> *I was at FSU and my roommate, Robin, began babysitting the girls. She would come home and tell stories about these beautiful toddler girls. I would help her out when she was unable to make it. They (Rick and Donna) had to have a troop of babysitters available because they were so busy socially. The girls were spunky and had their own personalities. Madi always seemed like the Daddy's girl, loving being outside and taking on anything that came along. Callie was more demure, but had her own little rebellious streak too. Donna liked to have me over because I played non-stop with the girls. They had a lot of Rick in them, energy wise.*

*Donna kept the schedule and behind the scenes doing all the regular stuff. She was the consistent one trying to keep up with his calendar. Rick would come in, get the girls riled up, and then be off again. The girls couldn't get enough of him. I don't know if it was because I was in college, but looking at Rick and Donna was to me like looking at the Kennedys. Beautiful mom, charismatic dad, happy little girls. Life was good.*

When Rick and Donna later divorced in 2005, his time with his daughters shortened, as happens in most cases of shared custody. But his love and pride in them was unbridled and he spoke of them often to anyone who would listen, as a fellow attorney at Morgan & Morgan observed:

*He loved his girls. Without reservation. Without ANY reservation. When he spoke of them he literally glowed with love. I hope they both realize at some later point that whatever the issues between him and their mother, he would have given his last dollar or breath to give either of those girls whatever they needed. They were loved. They never need to lay awake at night and wonder. They were loved with a magnificent passion.*

Even though they had both moved on in their lives, Rick regularly expressed his guilt and regret for the marriage breaking up to many of his friends:

*My favorite quote from him was, "Never leave the first wife." He said that on the second or third bourbon one night in Orlando. He said his biggest regret was he and Donna breaking up. Rick was always a wanderer. Feared emotion and commitment and once things started getting good he had to screw it up. He enjoyed having a family unit, but at the end of the day he was like his dad and not capable of being a one woman man. If he had been, the divorce from Donna would have been the catalyst for him to change. He was very sad and you could see how much he was missing his children.*

My husband would occasionally stop by the law office on a lunch break just to see me and say hello. When he was leaving, he'd always give me a kiss and a big hug and tell me that he loved me. Rick would witness this and come into my office after David left. "How long have you two been together?" he'd ask. "Twenty-five years," I replied. "That's amazing! I wish I could meet someone that I'd want to slobber over after twenty-five years." "It's not in your DNA." I hated myself as soon as I'd say something like that to him, because I knew it hurt him to think that he would never find happiness in a committed relationship.

The only thing Rick ever said to me about his divorce from Donna was that he never thought something that didn't really mean that much to him (an affair with another woman) would cause him to lose the one thing that was the most precious to him. He said something similar to a friend who stayed with Rick after he and his wife separated:

> *I stayed with him for a short while when I was going through my dark side and he had his dark side. We were not good for each other. All we did was cry on each other's shoulders and drink ourselves to sleep each night. He didn't give me any advice other than to tell me to look at him and don't do what he did. He said it wasn't worth the pain to not make things work.*

As he advanced up the legal ladder, Rick eventually landed in Tallahassee where he became a partner in a prestigious, multi-state civil law firm. Although he was licensed to practice law in Florida, Georgia, and Texas, he chose Florida's capital city because of its opportunities in private and government litigation, and for the close proximity to his family's land holdings in Georgia. He earned a reputation as a no nonsense litigator who was a bulldog with no backup to him. If he took a bite, there was no shaking loose. He won some cases he should have lost, but once he set his sights on winning, you had no chance.

Despite the fact that his client pool was massive and provided exposure to an elite group of admirers, he eventually became disenchanted with the politics of working in a big system. "All they care about is billing and amassing large client lists, but they don't give a shit about anyone or anything if a large retainer ain't connected to it," he'd often tell me. Thus, he ventured out on his own and set up the Bateman Harden law firm. I asked him about the Harden part and he said it was a family name. I couldn't understand why there wasn't a person attached to the name in the firm. "I don't believe in naming a law firm or any company after just yourself," he said. "It sounds too egotistical, and besides, some people might not like Rick Bateman, but would think there's another guy whose name is on the card that they would be comfortable with," he'd muse. "So, there is no Harden associated with Bateman Harden?" I asked. "Nope."

A second time at the marriage altar came in 2007, after a whirlwind courtship with Bridgette Mitchell. Young, darkly beautiful, and recently divorced with two young sons, Bridgette was the yin to Rick's yang. He was crazy about her to the point of distraction. They were set up for a blind date by a mutual friend, who knew they would hit it off, but couldn't predict just how well:

> *I knew Bridgette when she was married to John and was commuting from Cairo, Georgia to work as a nail tech at the same salon where I was doing massages. I lost track of her for a little while, but then she turned up at my gynecologist's office as a nurse assistant. I asked her how she was and she told me about her divorce, and about her dating a guy who had just died of a drug overdose. It had been just a couple of months since that had happened and she said she wasn't ready to start dating anyone else just yet. I knew she was Rick's type physically, and she was fun. I knew they were made for each other. I told her I had a guy she would be perfect for and to let me know when*

*she was ready. I'd set Rick up with several of my friends actually.*

*Not much later she texted me and said she was ready. I gave Rick her number and they met. Within two weeks they were ridiculous and would leave me messages about how happy they were. I told them I knew they would get along, but whatever they did with it was on them. I warned her that Rick was out there and to proceed with caution. But no, she just stampeded in.*

The marriage lasted just months. "She was my greatest passion, but we were too needy with each other," Rick told me sadly. "I couldn't live with her and I feel that I can't live without her." Even though the legal union was broken, they remained in one another's lives. Rick made sure to set up a college fund for her sons in addition to paying for health care for all of them. He referred to her as "B" and they constantly texted their feelings in code to one another. A lot of people told Rick that Bridgette was an impediment to any future happiness he might have with another woman, since he wouldn't let go of his unhealthy desire to have her in his life. I was never surprised when he would show up with Bridgette with him, even after she had moved to Seagrove Beach near Destin and was living in his beach house there. They seemed so natural together and it pained me to watch the fights they had more often than not. He memorialized his feelings for her when he amended his Will to include her as his only beneficiary apart from his daughters. It proved to be an empty gesture as debtors lined up ahead of her for their share of his life insurance proceeds. In the end, she got a framed sketch of the house on Sixth Avenue he had bequeathed to her that was verging on foreclosure, and a lot of memories.

Rick loved excellence in all things, but hadn't a clue of how to care for or maintain them. He knew where to buy expensive Cuban cigars in New York City when he worked or visited there, but would absent mindedly leave boxes of them in the back of taxis. He was familiar with every style of Rolex watch and gifted them to lovers. I watched in horror as he threw one of his own across the conference room after a fight on the phone with Bridgette. He dressed in the finest Savelle Row shirts and Canali suits, but would think nothing of putting a fountain pen in a chest pocket and cause blue ink to indelibly stain them. He bought the best fishing tackle, hunting gear, sunglasses and clothing, some of which smelled of mildew and still had store stickers on them when I found them during the clean out of his closets after his death. He was a lifelong fan of Ford trucks, always buying the biggest and most tricked out model on the market. They were always a mess...nail clippers hanging from the mirror, clothes, money, guns, files, and golf balls strewn everywhere. One time, he and a friend were driving to Georgia and a putrid smell in the truck was making his friend sick. Rick reached down under his seat and pulled out a bag of old boiled peanuts, which proved to be the source of the foul odor. "They must be from last season when I went duck hunting," Rick offered nonchalantly.

He was a voracious reader and eager tourist whenever visiting new places. He knew, for instance, that there are over thirty different kinds of marble in the floors and walls of the Waldorf Astoria. He was generous to a fault with friends who knew he had access to many theater and sports events. He would gladly give away fourth row-center seat tickets to a Broadway show if it made a friend look like a big shot in his girlfriend's eyes - or use his influence to acquire sold out concert tickets for a father to impress his daughters:

> *He never saw a tab he did not want to pick up. He hosted random outings to bars, all at his full expense, and had more fun than anyone else there. When my two college girls at FSU wanted to go see some rapper named Drake, Rick got me tickets through his connections at the Leon County Civic Center. He had to put the tickets on his American Express. When I e-mailed him days later asking for the details to reimburse him, I told him my daughters thought I was a hero for scoring the tickets. He e-mailed me back, "Damn right you are a hero!" I never did get any reimbursement information from him. My efforts to pick up his bar tabs as some quid pro quo were rebuffed constantly.*

Golfing, horse racing, luxury European cars, twelve-year-old single malt Scotch whiskey, and women were among his favorite things. All of these required lots of money. His obsession for amassing huge sums of it supplanted all other loves, and was the one that began his fall from grace.

*Rick's identity and sense of self worth was dependent on being a financial success. It wasn't the money, but the image and his ego. I'd go fishing with him. He didn't like fishing, but he liked the image of the boat. He didn't like hunting, but he liked being Rick Bateman, outdoorsman.*

*When things went downhill financially, he couldn't bear it. Rick was an extraordinarily gifted lawyer. If he'd focused all his attention on that he would never have had anything to worry about. It was the art of the deal that attracted him. The American dream has become doing as little as possible for as much as you can get. Rick always wanted to hit a home run, never a single and get on base. When the market was going up, that worked. But that same mentality is what stings you when the market goes down.*

Rick lived and breathed to practice law. He enjoyed the largesse of clients' fees and court settlements, but what really made his juices flow was being a trail-blazer for application of arcane statutes against some very serious opposition. To some, he was ruthless; to others, he was fearless. He always gave better than he got.

The bottom line was that people either loved him or hated him. I didn't care what others thought, I knew he had a good heart. People who hated him only saw the outside aggressive, womanizer side. They didn't know he was, as a close friend observed, "Just a shit covered jelly roll." Once you got through the shit, you saw how sweet he really was.

# Chapter 2

## *Meet Rick Bateman*

Rick Bateman and I came together through a series of circumstances that can only be called kismet. I had semi-retired in my mid-fifties from an executive career of non-profit management. My husband and I were dividing our time between Tallahassee and New Smyrna Beach, where we were remodeling beach houses for resale and enjoying the seemingly non-stop ascent of real estate appreciation. The satisfaction of taking a barren white stucco tear down and turning it into the prettiest house on the block was fun at first, but proved to be short lived fulfillment for me. I realized that I was too young and too bored to continue on this path. I needed a career challenge, but I wasn't willing to go full tilt boogey back into the management/lobbying lifestyle from which I had retired. My ego no longer needed to be salved by taking charge of a company or association, meeting with leaders of industry, and delegating assignments to a large staff. I wanted a job where I could be second banana to someone who would seek and appreciate the wisdom of my experience and insight, and use them to help formulate their own leadership.

One late fall day while laying pavers in the hot sun at the last house we would market, I was mentally debating the idea of returning to daily employment. I received a phone call from my friend, Marjorie, whose legislative campaign I had managed and who had since moved on to become President of the Tallahassee Community College (TCC) Foundation. She was planning an extravaganza to be the culmination of a major fundraising campaign for the foundation and wanted me to coordinate the event. I jumped at the opportunity to dip my toe into some creative waters again. We sold our little pink cottage on the beach in one day for a handsome profit, packed up our things, and headed back to Tallahassee.

I had three months to pull it off, so all my energies were concentrated on the production. The ceremony would be a combination of an American Indian tribal ceremony and the Academy Awards! What can I say? If nothing else, I'm eclectic! I spent countless hours selecting the talent, recording the music, obtaining the costumes, writing the scripts, choreographing the event, and selecting the menu. I decided to give the board of directors a taste of what was in store at their meeting one week before the big event. Several of them were chosen to play a role in a greatly abbreviated musical number. It was hilarious to see a bank president, a civil engineer, and a brain surgeon sing a parody to the Brooks & Dunn song, "Play Something Country!" The skit and the awards banquet were both big hits.

Fast forward two months. Marjorie called me one day and asked what I was doing. One of her board members who had participated in my little preview was looking for an Executive Assistant. His current one was moving out of town and he needed someone mature with great organizational skills to replace her. Marjorie wanted to know if I was interested. I said yes, but I have to admit that I secretly worried that I would be able to actually be an assistant. I had been the top dog in charge for many years. It wasn't that I thought the position beneath me - quite the contrary. I had been blessed with some incredible administrative assistants in my time and they were worth their weight in gold! It's just that I'm so action oriented that I worried I would over step my bounds and get myself in trouble while making my boss look bad.

After a couple of days of soul searching, I agreed to an interview. The job was with a large civil engineering firm, Moore Bass Consulting, as Rick Moore's Executive Assistant. To be honest, I didn't remember that much about Rick Moore from my brief time at the TCC gig, but I figured I would find out what I needed at the interview. As it turned out, I never met with him. After a brief interview with the company's chief operations officer, I was asked if I would consider working in the engineering division across the street with one of the company's rising engineering stars heading up the firm's work on some big projects. I was taken aback and said I'd have to think about it. I was told the young engineer was out of town, but would be back in a few days and would I be willing to come back and meet with him. I left thinking that this really wasn't what I had wanted to do and I probably would just say no when they called again. I knew nothing of engineering. What in the world would I be expected to do and how would my previous executive/lobbying experience be utilized?

I did agree to go back, if for no other reason than to satisfy my curiosity about what this Moore Bass group did operationally. From the moment I walked in the conference room and shook hands with Clay Campbell, I knew this was where I was meant to be. Something instinctual just told me that Clay and I would be good friends and do great things together. He was in his early forties, married with two young children and one on the way. He was a Kappa Alpha fraternity guy from Florida State University and had a killer sense of humor. All of the "engineers in training" idolized him. He was smart, funny, and knew when someone needed encouragement or direction. He managed several of the firm's major contracts, including the controversial Fallschase development, on which he had daily interaction with elected officials of the city and county to negotiate the plans for the mammoth commercial and residential project on behalf of his client, Lamar Bailey.

Bailey, a well-known luminary of real estate development in Leon County, had acquired 700 acres of property along Buck Lake Road in Tallahassee over a twelve year period of time. He named the development Fallschase and came up with the concept of the area having its own special taxing district modeled on Reedy Creek at Disney World. It would be a quasi governmental entity with the power to levy taxes, fees, etc. to fund the infrastructure. Originally, there was little commercial activity anticipated, but when the county took away most of Bailey's other development rights, the commercial activity grew. The economy was the major enemy of getting the project going. The district was approved and bonds were sold to build Phase I, a 150 unit subdivision. Five or six houses were constructed as models of what was to come. Then, the nation's financial crisis of the 1970s stalled everything and the project languished until 1997, pleasing many environmental enthusiasts who saw the project as a denigration of the natural resources in the area.

Recognizing the political difficulties he was having with water, sewer and floodplain issues, Bailey sought the best and brightest talent to modify the Fallschase project to make it more palatable to the naysayers. Lee Vause, a retired Leon County Commissioner, was one of the talents he was determined to acquire.

*Lamar tried for two years to get me to help him, but I didn't want to get involved because I had retired and didn't want to take on anything that ambitious. Finally, I agreed to attend commission meetings and coordinate some of the ongoing dialogue, since the state was fighting the DRI (Development of Regional Impact) designation. I met with all of Lamar's attorneys, reviewed all the filings and documents from the preceding twenty years, and worked with the county legal office to determine a site specific zoning within the county's comprehensive plan. Clay Campbell at Moore Bass was key in getting Fallschase labeled as a Planned Unit Development (PUD), which isn't a zoning designation, but a contract with the county laying out what can and can't be part of the development.*

*I recommended Rick Bateman to be part of the legal team. He became the mouthpiece for Fallschase to the county commission. I had been on the commission when Rick began lobbying in addition to doing legal work. I don't remember the first time he came before us, but I had recommended him as an attorney to half a dozen people over the years, sometimes for business before the commission and other times something else. I had no problem recommending him for items coming before us, not because I agreed with him, but because the client needed a champion to bring their issue to the fore, and he was definitely that guy. I admired his tenacity and sheer bulldogging to help his client win the day. I knew he'd be great for the Fallschase team because he had the ability to say to Lamar, "You're wrong", when it was necessary, and Lamar wasn't an easy person to say that to.*

I had been working with Clay for a week or so when a hot wind blew into my office in the form of a man, over six feet tall and unbent, with a full head of jet black hair slicked back, and dressed in black shorts and windbreaker, sneakers, and reading glasses dangling from a cord around his neck. In an instant, I was picked up from my chair by this human hurricane and assaulted with a wet kiss directly on my mouth, then dropped back into my chair as his tailwinds swept by and into Clay's office through an adjoining door. Before I could comprehend what had just happened, the smooth drawl of Clay called out without punctuation, "Jude, meet Rick Bateman."

The next two years were such a joy for me. Clay relied on me more and more and we spent long hours in his office sharing stories of political successes, Fallschase strategies, and our common bond – cancer. I had fought my battle many years before and had the disease on the run, but Clay's was ongoing. He had seen many doctors and the disease went into remission for a brief time, only to return with a vengeance less than a year later. Despite his pain, he worked tirelessly on his engineering projects and always made time to horse around with the dozens of staff under his direction. Rick Bateman added to our good times, coming around frequently to review changes to the Fallschase plans to share with county staff and to check on Clay, who he loved like a brother. They often went fishing together and made ridiculous bets on who caught the biggest fish, who caught the most fish, or who told the best fishing story.

The Fallschase project was finally approved, thanks in no small part to Rick's ability to twist arms to his favor on new and controversial issues. From my lobbying days, I knew it was much easier to kill a bill than to get new legislation passed, so I especially admired Rick's talents in that regard. So did a developer who attended many of those public hearings:

> *I met him when he was at the top of the mountain. The air was thin and he was the king of the hill. He never had to do his homework. He'd just walk in and argue the hell out of something and everyone would go along with it.*

Not everyone was immediately impressed with Rick as legal counsel to the project. After the development received its PUD status, Bailey sold the entire project to AIG Baker. They tapped a former St. Joe Paper executive to manage the project:

> *I had been hired by AIG Baker to lead the team of professionals who were brought in to design and permit the Fallschase project. One of the first times Rick and I worked together, we were walking downtown from his office to the courthouse where he would be presenting one of our plans to the Commission. It always made me*

*laugh that he didn't care how he looked as an attorney. He'd wear an Izod polo shirt buttoned up all the way under a random suit jacket (not a blazer), with khakis, loafers and no socks. His hair always looked like he just got out of bed. As we were walking, I noticed a piece of freezer tape rolled up in the back of his shoe. "What's that on your heel?" "I ran out of band aids and just grabbed some freezer tape to put back there 'cause I have this damn blister." I thought to myself, "Really? This is the attorney you guys brought to the table?!"*

*He could have been a master of disguise. His facial expressions and how he dressed would sometimes fool even me when I saw him. He didn't really give a shit about what people thought about him. He just made you feel good being around him. There was always an excitement because you never knew what he was going to say or what deal he was about to rope you into.*

The day finally came when Clay could no longer come to the office in order to devote all his time to fighting his battle with cancer. I thought the silence would kill me. I would stand in his doorway looking at his desk, and wishing so hard that he would magically appear behind it as the young, vibrant man I had seen that first day. My melancholy was interrupted by a phone call. It was Rick Bateman. He was calling to see how I was doing and wanted to meet me after work for a drink. I begged off, knowing how late the evenings can get when Rick was buying the drinks! I lived an hour south of Tallahassee and driving that long distance in the dark with a few drinks under my belt was not something I wanted to test. I worked late and was one of the last to leave the building. Rick, not being one to take no for an answer, was standing in the parking lot with a bottle of wine in his hand. I don't know how long he had been waiting out there and I told him how surprised I was to see him. "I thought we should drink a toast to Clay kicking cancer's ass!" he shouted. It was the first time I'd laughed like that in a long while. We sat in my car and took turns taking swigs from the bottle of a very good, and very expensive Cabernet Sauvignon while I was entertained with stories of Rick's hunting and fishing adventures.

Rick Moore and Karen Bass took me under their wing for a year after Clay stopped coming to work. He was a partner in the firm and they said that I was now, de facto, their partner in his absence. They wanted to support me in any way to keep Clay's work on the books so he could continue receiving his partner share. I don't think I ever respected and admired two people more than at that moment. It was around this time that the real estate investment bubble had burst. The impact was felt by countless individuals and companies, including the Moore Bass firm. Dozens of engineering professionals and staff in their branch offices in Florida and Georgia, as well as the Tallahassee main office, were being laid off. A skeleton crew would remain to ride out the hard times and hopefully, grow back to a bigger and better operation when the economy steadied itself. I was one of the last to be let go, and even then Rick and Karen bent over backwards to make my exit as painless as possible. Clay took it hard and cried when I saw him afterward. I told him I was fine and that he needed to concentrate on himself. A week later, Rick Bateman called me and offered me a job.

# Chapter 3

## *Shock & Awe*

The elevator in the old bank building stalled between floors. I was on my way to see Rick in his office on the top floor to discuss the job he had offered me. I thought the stalled elevator was a fitting metaphor for my situation. I really liked Rick, but how in the world could I work for someone so completely opposite of Clay? Clay was a gentleman. Rick was not. Clay was quiet. Rick was loud. Clay was funny. Rick was profane. Clay was respectful. Rick was bawdy. *Oh well,* I thought. *I really don't need this job, so what the heck, enjoy the interview.* When I finally got to his suite of offices, no one was there to greet me. I had to walk around to find his governmental assistant who waved to me to go into Rick's office. As it turned out, Rick's long time secretary had resigned weeks before and the office was now piled high with paperwork and files. Rick gave me a big hug when he saw me and slammed the door behind me. "Jude, please come work with me and manage my life!" he begged. "I need your organizational skills and your intellect to make this place look like a professional law firm. I'll pay you whatever you want." When I told him my price, he sputtered, "Well, that's more than I pay some of my lawyers!" I told him that was too bad and stood up to leave. "Wait!" he screamed. "Can't we work out a deal?" "Mr. Bateman, I don't deal about my worth," I said. The phone rang, Rick took the call, and I let myself out. "Thank, God!" I said out loud on the stairs (I chose to avoid the elevator this time). "There's no way I could work with that man and now I don't have to worry about it!" Two days later he agreed to my terms and I was now employed by Bateman Harden law firm.

On my first day at work, no one seemed to know what my job was going to be or where I was going to sit. It was assumed I'd sit where Rick's secretary had sat, so I weaved my way between notebooks and files stacked on the floor and found the chair loaded with loose papers and sheets of file labels. Rick was in court and not expected until noon. Sheri, the firm's paralegal, gave me some pointers about the phones and a list of cases, but said she really didn't know anything more about what I was going to do. I spent the morning looking through files to familiarize myself with names of clients in case any of them called. A florist delivered a beautiful arrangement to me. They were from Clay with a note to, "Spread sunshine as only you can." I looked at the cold, grey November sky outside and thought of him reaching out to me in his darkest hours to make me feel better about my new and alien work environment. I wanted to bolt from the office and crawl under a warm blanket at home, but was jolted back to reality by a very loud, "Jude!"

Rick was walking down the hall with another man behind him. "So, you showed up!" he said smiling broadly. "Meet Jeff Bradley. He's one of our clients and just pissed off the attorney representing those bastards in Dixie County!" he declared proudly. "Nice to meet you, Mr. Bradley," I said stretching out my hand. "It's Jeff!" Rick scolded from his office. Jeff never said a word and just followed Rick into his office. Rick slammed the door, which was only five feet in front of the desk behind which I was barricaded. I could feel the vibration of the wood shuddering from the hit. Sheri put a call through to his office and the verbal assault with the caller began in earnest. During the next five minutes, I heard every foul and profane word known to man and beast. The volume and tempre of his voice reached a crescendo on each "Fuck you!" and my ears, nose and throat felt as though they had been scraped raw. Rick opened and slammed the door shut again, this time with even more gusto than before. Papers on my desk flew off from the wind gust.

The case involved a stop work order imposed on the housing development our client had permitted with Dixie County. After approving the planned residential development, the county ruled that the development was not in conformity with its Land Use Regulations and would not allow the project to move forward. Rick argued that the county's action was an inverse condemnation, or a "taking," of the land from the developer and those individuals who had pre-purchased lots. The case was eventually settled after it came to light that the county's attorney had absconded with hundreds of thousands of dollars of our client's funds and others that should have been deposited in escrow as bonds for projects. Rick assisted the FBI in their prosecution of the county attorney, who was eventually found guilty in federal court on nineteen counts, including the one involving our client's development, and sent to federal prison.

When the meeting concluded and Jeff left, I walked into Rick's office and sat down in front of him. He was on his cell phone, delighting someone with the details of his just-finished "ass kicking" of that "pecker wood" of an attorney.

He looked up at me and saw that I wasn't smiling and cut the call short. "What's up?" he said. "I don't think this is going to work," I told him. "My senses have been assaulted and I am literally in pain right now from the verbal tirade you just had. I'm not used to this kind of behavior in a professional setting. I think it's best for me to leave and for you to find someone else." "Wait a minute, Jude! I'm sorry if you're hurting, but we need to have an understanding. You're right...I need to be better about cussing all the time and I promise to try. In fact, I want you to tell me when I step over the line. But, at the same time, you need to cut me some slack when I'm dealing with other attorneys or anyone on the other side in a case." I was not convinced, but listening. "Law is like war. You got to intimidate the other side in order to get them to back off. If they don't back off, you got to hit them with all the ammunition you got. I don't yell at folks for the fun of it! I yell at them because I'm fighting for the rights of my clients and I know that they need me to stand up for them." "Okay," I said. "I'll give you that berth if you agree to tone down your cursing in front of me." "Deal!" he said laughing.

Without really saying anything, Rick and I came to an understanding of how far each of us could go with the other. He liked to impose his will as long as people would let him. Most people were afraid of him and not confident enough to go against him. He fed off of that. I started working in my teens and had come up against just about every type of personality out there. The one time I had let my guard down, as far as standing up for myself, was in my first marriage and it nearly cost me my life. When I finally released my fear from that experience, I regained my strength of character and vowed I would never let anyone intimidate or dominate me again. When Rick pushed me too hard, I would push back with calm firmness. When I got a little too bossy with him, he'd call me "Missy". "You might want to back off a bit, Missy!" he'd say looking over his glasses and I knew it was time to bite my lip and leave the room. I was perfect for him because he never upset me. He upset others he worked with, but I always reconciled Rick by what was expected. A former partner shared his own experience with Rick's acerbic office behavior:

> *He was what I expected in a brilliant way. I thought he was adorable. To be Rick's partner is to not change him, but to follow him around with a hose because his hair is on fire! He was always going 100 miles per hour.*

> *I hated the way he talked to the people who worked for him. He always got results, but it bothered me. I think in the early years he attracted a lot of people who didn't have a lot of self respect, because no one who did would listen to what he said to them. I think as he grew more sophisticated, he decided he would surround himself with real talent. Watching that change over the years was a beautiful thing.*

There were two times I witnessed firsthand how the wild horse in Rick tried to stomp over two friends and business associates, and how each one artfully put the bit in his mouth:

*We got into an argument in his office that spilled out to the parking lot. We were going at it pretty good and he finally told me that I had to leave because no one spoke to him like that in his office. As people were driving in and out of the lot, they were giving me the thumbs up as if to say, "Yay! Somebody's finally putting him in his place!" I looked at him and said, "So, is this how this is going to end between us?" He said, no, he was just having a bad day and I should know that's how he was. I told him he needed to quit that shit because someday he'd push someone too far. Without fail, he would always bring up that fight when we were together socially and tell people about how I stood up to him.*

~~~~~

*We had been on the phone, yelling obscenities at each other. He had defaulted on a loan I'd given him and after trying every which way but Sunday to give him a chance to repay me, he tells me to go to hell and he'll kick my ass. I told him there was no fence around my ass and I'd just as soon kick his. So, I jump in my car and drive over to his office. He's in an important client meeting and looks out and sees me. He excused himself and came out and got in my face, trying to dance me out on the front porch to get me out of the building. I told him he hadn't met his obligations and if I wasn't a friend, he'd be in a lot more trouble than I was giving him. He mumbled something and told me he'd call me later. I left and we eventually worked everything out. But it hurt me the way he treated me, calling me a bully. We were never really the same with each other after that.*

Clay lost his battle with cancer on February 11, 2009, just one week after his forty-sixth birthday. I had seen him almost daily in the weeks leading up to his death, but it was still devastating news when I got the e-mail from his sister that he had passed in the night. On one of my last visits, he asked me if I would speak at his funeral. I now had to call on all my inner strength and resources to put something together that would honor him. Standing at the podium in that huge church full of friends and family, all of whom were feeling the same sense of loss as I, the words I had written came out easily at first. Then I looked down and saw the fishing rod that Clay's father had propped against his casket and I lost it. I struggled to fight back the sobs and finish my words of love for Clay. When the proceedings were finally over, I turned to my husband and said that I wanted to get out of there as quickly as possible because I knew I still had many tears that needed to flow. As I stood up, I felt my body go limp. From out of nowhere, Rick Bateman had plowed through the crowd and hugged me so ferociously that it took my breath away. He sobbed with me and only let me go when

Bridgette, his second ex-wife and forever lover, tapped him on the back and told him they had to go see the family.

The following Monday, I was at my desk when Rick arrived and asked me to come into his office. He was still wearing his overcoat and looked horrible. He hadn't shaved and I could tell he hadn't slept for a while. He closed the door and pulled his chair in front of mine. Leaning over, he took both of my hands in his. "Jude, I want to confide something to you, **only** you, and I know you'll understand. I can't get Clay out of my mind and I can't get his funeral out of my mind. God, there were so many people there and they all loved and respected him so much." I sat there quietly, a little nervous at where this was going. Rick squeezed my hands and started to cry. He looked directly at me and said softly, "I want what Clay had. I want to be a better person. I need you to help me; I have a problem. I'm going to go to Alcoholics Anonymous and I wanted you to know that." He then sat back in his chair and looked at me with those soulful brown eyes, like a little boy waiting to be told he was doing the right thing. "Rick, I think it's admirable that you recognize you have a problem and that you are going to do something about it. But, you alone are responsible for your actions and the only one who can change them. I can't do it. No one can. I will pray for you and be here to talk with you whenever you want to, but I can't make you go to meetings and I can't make you stop doing bad things to yourself." He stared at me for a moment and then stood up and thanked me for listening to him. We never discussed it again and I don't know how many meetings he attended. But, based on his last years of life, I know he didn't stop doing bad things to himself.

# Chapter 4

## *Rick Gone Wild*

"Be careful what you wish for!" I cautioned Rick after he announced that he'd just finished a conference call with a lawyer in California about our firm representing Joe Francis, the infamous producer of "Girls Gone Wild" videos. While I hadn't actually seen any of the videos, I had seen their promotion on "E! Entertainment" channel. The concept of college co-eds baring their breasts for a filmed spring break thrill seemed sad and disgusting to me. Joe Francis took the filming to a heightened level and began packaging and distributing the videos to a worldwide audience, making him a very rich man. Along the way, he had been sued by a number of young women who accused him of taking liberties with their filmed antics without their permission. Most recently, he was being accused by a group of young women of violating the Federal and Florida RICO statutes by videotaping minors in sexually explicit conduct and distributing those videos. Joe was currently sitting in a jail in Panama City and facing serious time for his contempt of the judicial system in not making himself or his companies' records available to the court.

"What are you talking about?!" Rick responded incredulously to my warning. "This will be a great case for us and we'll get lots of free publicity in the process!" Rick was always looking for an opportunity to promote himself. "If they ain't talking about you, good or bad, you ain't doing anything worthwhile," he'd often say. He had personally amassed a contact list of over 10,000 people, inclusive of private cell phone numbers of celebrities and elites, which everyone coveted. Many times I received phone calls from his friends asking for a cell phone number for someone important. I would always decline and advise that I'd let Rick know they needed it, to which they quickly withdrew their request!

I printed out our standard retainer agreement and took it into Rick for review. He made some minor, but crafty changes that would prove useful in court years later when Joe stopped paying us. The retainer was executed through electronic mail and by the end of the day, Bateman Harden was the legal firm representing Joe Francis and his companies in the case of Plaintiff B, et. al. v Joseph R. Francis, et. al. in U. S. District Court. And, Rick was right as usual...the first story broke in the *Tallahassee Democrat* just one week later:

> "*A Tallahassee civil attorney has been hired to represent the creator of the 'Girls Gone Wild' video series in a federal lawsuit that claims the company exploited underage girls by filming them exposing their breasts and engaging in sexually explicit conduct.*
>
> *Rick Bateman, who has lived and worked in Tallahassee for more than two decades, took on the case recently, although the suit was filed in*

*Panama City in March 2008. Bateman said he and his client, Joseph R. Francis, intend to go to trial, which is set for July.*

*'They didn't want to hire a hometown lawyer, but they didn't want to pick someone from Chicago or L.A. either,' Bateman said, explaining why he was picked. Bateman is a prominent, politically connected attorney whose specializations include government relations and development issues.*

*A former Florida State University student who said she was filmed exposing her breasts in New Orleans without her consent settled privately in 2002 with Francis' companies, M.R.A. Holdings and Mantra Films.*

*Bateman said his client has asked District Judge Richard Smoak in Panama City to recuse himself, since he's the one who sentenced Francis in 2007 to thirty-five days behind bars for criminal contempt during a similar civil suit.*

*'He believes that he had to settle that case based on the duress and coercion of being in jail and not being able to get out of the jail,' Bateman said."*

When our representation began, we had just one paralegal, Sheri, and two lawyers (including Rick) to work on the Francis case in addition to the dozens of other cases we had underway. The two firms hired to represent the four Plaintiffs had offices in Chicago, New York, Los Angeles, Miami, and Panama City, and boasted legions of lawyers, paralegals, and investigators on their staffs. We were bombarded daily with copious legal filings, all of which required a response in detail for each of the legal offices copied on the pleadings. It was also around this time that federal courts began electronic filing of all court documents, and our staff had to quickly learn the ropes on the filing rules. Because we had received a large deposit on the agreed retainer fee from Joe's office, Rick began in earnest the hunt for additional legal talent to join our firm for this high profile case. Over the next two years, we burned through four attorneys, six interns, two runners, and eight paralegals, all of whom I had to interview, hire, and in some cases, fire. By the time we withdrew from the exhausting and sometimes frustrating representation, we were reduced to two attorneys (including Rick), one intern, one paralegal, and one runner. Even with limited resources, Rick not only held his own against the larger firms with their seemingly endless supply of legal talent, he had them "balls to the wall" and put the fear of Bateman in opposing counsel.

Six months after taking the Francis case, Rick decided he wanted to buy a law office building and vacate the suite of offices we had been renting downtown. "We need room to expand," he would say to me while throwing countless files on the floor next to his desk. In addition to the Bateman Harden work, Rick owned over twenty corporations that he ran out of our office, most of them set up to shelter the property acquisitions he had made. After weeks of researching real estate listings, Rick announced one day that he had brokered a deal to buy the Chesley House, just three blocks from our downtown offices. It was a beautiful, historic building that occupied the corner of Gadsden and Virginia Streets, with lots of gingerbread trim along the front gables and a white picket fence bordering the property. We doubled our office and storage space, but the relocation would prove to be one of the worst real estate decisions Rick ever made. As I feared, the actual move fell on my shoulders. Rick was busy with court appearances and the rest of the staff magically disappeared when it came time to unpack and organize the offices on Friday afternoon. *As God is my witness, this will be the last time I move this law office!* I swore to myself as the moving company dumped boxes and furniture helter skelter, while I waited for computers to be set up and telephone service men to arrive two hours after their scheduled appointments. But, we were up and running on Monday morning with minimal hiccups to our business operation.

"Jude! Where the hell is my hotel reservation for tonight?!" Rick was yelling from across the hall. I had dreamt of my office being the one just down the hall from his with a crystal chandelier and two storage closets. I had suffered with the cramped space in our previous location and he promised that I could "have the pick of the litter" in our new offices. But, I had to give up my fantasy of a dream office in order to give Rick direct contact with me. He needed me to be within eyesight of him so we could communicate without intercom, and that meant setting up in the small room across the hall from his spacious one, complete with a working fireplace and private entrance. I was his touchstone every time he had a phone call or a client meeting and needed me to mouth confirmation of something, or for me to know from his side of a conversation if I needed to take something immediately to him for reference.

"Same hotel as last time," I assured him and pointed to the file containing his reservation information on his desk. "Cancel it!" he directed. "I'm staying somewhere else tonight and don't need it." I knew from the tone in his voice, as well as from a cell phone conversation I'd just overheard, that he would be staying at his Seagrove Beach house where he was letting his second ex-wife and her sons reside rent free. Bridgette and Rick were always "on again/off again." Theirs was a volatile, passionate relationship that would torture him until the day he died, and cost him the friendship of at least one long time associate who shared, "Some of the darkness with Bridgette and what he did to himself made it impossible in the end to be with him."

This particular trip to Panama City was for the videotaped deposition of Joe Francis by the Plaintiffs' counsels. Rick was concerned that the session would go long and he would be unable to corral Joe for such an extended period of time without incident. His client's behavior was frenzied at best and it was ironic to watch Rick, who I likened to a nerve ending, playing the calming father figure to Joe. He decided to have another strong male in attendance with him, so he asked a retired law enforcement friend who was now an international consultant on security and enforcement, to ride along with Sheri and him to the deposition.

*I was walking through Beall's one day and*
*all of a sudden someone comes up from behind*

*and shoves me. I whipped around (Rick would tell others that I went into a full Ninja stance, but that never happened). Rick laughed and we caught up with each other since I hadn't seen him for a few years. He told me about the Francis case and gave me the whole story about how the sheriff in the county where Joe's trial would be held had threatened to put Joe in jail if he ever came back into his county. Evidently, Joe had done some things during Spring Break that had raised the sheriff's ire. Well, Joe did go back, got thrown in jail, and after that was petrified to travel to Florida. Rick said he needed to have Joe deposed in Panama City and knew he had to mitigate the situation with law enforcement. He told me he had immediately thought of me. We consummated the deal right then and there.*

*I went with Rick and Sheri to Panama City. We had the deposition in the afternoon and I stayed off of Joe's right shoulder and didn't say much. He was a piece of work…hadn't seen anything like him before. No police ever showed up. I think Joe's perception of what was going to happen was different from what was really happening. I had heard that the judge had told Rick that because he was now Joe's counsel, he was going to let some of Joe's past bad behavior slide.*

*A little later in the case, I was prepped to go to Mexico to meet with Joe. Rick needed him back in the states to participate in some hearings, but he had fallen off the radar. Rick found out he was in Mexico when Sheri told him she had seen him on some entertainment broadcast. I never did go. Right about that time was when Joe wasn't paying his bills and my role kind of died on the vine.*

From the very beginning of the deposition, Joe acted up. He would repeatedly burp and curse as the court reporter was setting up and refused to sit down until the filming was to begin. During the actual questioning of him, he would move from side to side and fart loudly after which he'd try to jump up to avoid further questioning. The actual video shows Rick's hand on one of Joe's shoulders with his friend's hand on Joe's other shoulder in an effort to keep him grounded. By the end of the deposition, Rick was visibly exhausted when a local news reporter interviewed him outside.

I was starting to get concerned that Rick was not giving enough attention to the other cases we had. He would give an intern the assignment of crafting a pleading and would ignore calls from clients in deference to his obsession with the Francis case. I confronted him with his lack of involvement with our caseload one day. My anger was fueled by the fact that Joe Francis had not paid us for costs we had carried for several months. "You are ignoring our good, paying clients who would appreciate a minute of your time to update them on the status of their cases!" I chided. "You do it!" he shot back. "I'm not their attorney! You are!" "God damn it, Jude! I've got to get this fucking response out the door by tomorrow and I don't have time to hold hands with a needy woman who likes to sue people as her hobby!" I glared at him for his use of profanity and for his lack of respect for a client I particularly liked and felt had an excellent case. But, he was already on his cell phone and making plans to meet with an expert we had hired in Gainesville for Joe's defense. I knew when to push him and when to withdraw, so I retreated to my office and stewed as I glanced at the calendar and saw that payroll was due to drop in two days and we didn't have the funds to cover it. I reluctantly picked up the phone and called clients (including the "needy woman" who Rick had disparaged) to ask for payments on their bills.

One day, about three months later, Rick came into my office and paced in front of my desk without saying a word. He had brilliantly won several major battles with the opposition in the Francis case, but he was losing patience with Joe's lack of attention to the growing bill he was amassing with our firm. I had used every opportunity I could to remind Rick of the balance outstanding so he would come to see how serious the situation was becoming. After a few minutes of pacing and looking at some of the framed artwork on my walls, he started to walk out without saying a word. "Did you want something?" I asked him. "No. I just wanted to think about something and I always find peace in your office," he said in a quiet monotone. I could tell that something was really eating at him, but he hadn't shared anything with me. He picked up his phone and called Joe's private cell number. It was almost 5:00 p.m. our time, so he was most likely hoping that Joe would be awake and answering his phone at 2:00 p.m. in Los Angeles. What happened next startled and delighted me. Rick fired Joe! He told him that he had all but won his case for him, but Joe had treated him with disrespect by ignoring our bills and we would no longer represent him until he caught up with his payments. Joe screamed profanities at Rick and hung up on him.

> *I think the reason that Rick allowed his representation to go on so long, even after Joe had stopped paying him, was because there was a part of Rick that wanted to be Joe. He identified with him on a level that most people couldn't, and I think that's what kept him in the game as long as he was. Even though he didn't like him as a guy or client, the fact that he built his female empire, Rick admired that. They were peas in a pod, although Joe was probably more certifiably crazier than Rick and was not as intelligent. Rick also had ethical parameters and Joe didn't.*

We ended up suing Joe for non-payment of fees and he counter-sued us for misuse of his funds. It took a couple of years to finally get an order from the court awarding us back fees and costs, but by then Joe had declared bankruptcy for his companies and we never collected any of the money. The saddest part is that Rick got the case ready for trial, but didn't get the credit. Joe decided to represent himself at the start of the trial, but in the eleventh hour another attorney was quickly hired to handle the final phase. She called Rick and he gave her his strategy and shared some of his drafted pleadings for her to use, all without expectation of any payment. When the case ended, her name was in the victory article. It became apparent shortly thereafter that a more serious defeat was the matter that bothered Rick that day he had come into my office. He had counted on our income from the Francis case to fund some of the recent investments he had made with money borrowed on the strength of our billings, most notably, the Francis ones. It also marked the beginning of Rick's decline as the wheeler dealer gunfighter that was the image that fueled him. He could forgive weakness in others, but not himself.

"Rick became a victim of a meteoric rise, had a great life, and then hit a wall and watched what he created evaporate. He couldn't maintain that level and that made him doubt himself. The loss of the Joe Francis money – he couldn't do what he promised everyone because of nonpayment," concluded a friend and creditor.

# Chapter 5

## *Water, Water Everywhere!*

Sometime in the middle of the Francis case, I received a phone call from Rick's maid  one Friday, asking if I could send our runner to his Millstone Plantation house to help her move the refrigerator so she could clean around it. She noticed a small puddle of water on the floor in front of it and wanted to take the opportunity to wash the entire kitchen area. Rick was in New York taking depositions and wouldn't be home until Monday. I dispatched our runner to the house and told him to stay there until the maid finished the floor so he could help her move the refrigerator back in place.

Rick owned several houses in and around Tallahassee, but was living in this one for now. It was the one he had bought for Bridgette when they got married, complete with a tree house he had built for the boys near the garage. The two-story, red brick house was impressive with stately white pillars out front, a circular drive with brick pavers surrounding a large fountain, and a saltwater swimming pool and tennis courts out back overlooking five rolling acres of hardwoods. The downstairs was furnished, but the second floor was not. After a brief marriage and an even briefer residency at the house, no time was spent furnishing the second story bedrooms. Since he traveled so much, Rick didn't occupy the house all that much anyway. I think he held onto it for the happy memories he had there with Bridgette and her boys. He knew he needed to sell it since it was a major liability on his personal financial statement. A good friend was interested in buying it and would be going by this particular weekend to walk through it with his wife in advance of putting an offer together.

Our runner came back to the office and reported that all was well. Everyone went home and looked forward to a peaceful weekend, knowing that Rick would be back on Monday and full of assignments on the Francis case. On Sunday, I received a phone call from Rick's friend who had viewed the house. He said that there was water all over the kitchen floor and the wallboard was stained as if it were also wet. He had taken the liberty of calling a plumber who had pulled up some of the molding below the wallboard and found water inside the wall. He did some investigating of the pipes under the house, but found no line breaks. I thanked him and hung up. *Great!* I thought. *There goes my Sunday!* I called Rick to warn him, but he didn't take my call. I figured further investigation of the issue could wait until the next morning, since Millstone was a good ninety minutes away and I wouldn't be able to get anyone out there on Sunday night anyway. I got on the computer and found a company that did flood mitigation work and figured they would be the best bet to give the place a thorough review. I tracked down the manager and called his cell phone. We agreed to meet at the house the following morning around 8:00 a.m.

Rick finally called me back late Sunday night when he was at the Atlanta airport for his connecting flight back to Tallahassee. I gave him a short rundown of the house issue and he said he'd wait to go to the office the next morning until I appeared so he could leave the house open. When I arrived at Millstone a few minutes before 8:00 a.m., the repairmen were already there, being entertained in the driveway by Rick who was dressed in his running outfit. "We got a real mess in there!" Rick yelled out to me as I got out of my car and walked toward the garage. He wasn't kidding. Water was an inch deep in the kitchen, pantry, family room, formal dining room, laundry room, master bedroom, and a child's bedroom down the hall. The walls were wet about halfway up and the floorboards were still exposed where the plumber had investigated the leak the night before. "Oh, my God!" was all that came out of me. Those beautiful Brazilian cherry plank floors were ruined. It was heartbreaking to see the devastation of the home. By now, the repair company manager was by my side giving me his report. "The icemaker hose broke away from the refrigerator and has been shooting a steady stream of water onto the wall behind it for at least a week," he said. The water had flowed down the wall and under the floors, then back up the wallboard. "Because the house is elevated, we were able to get under the floors and put down some barrier materials and fans to help dry it out down there," he told me. "How long will that take?" I asked. "About four or five days of constant running and we'll need to keep the air conditioning in the house running at least that long to keep the mildew out. All the furnishings will need to be taken out of the house and stored somewhere until all the repairs can be made." I was in shock and Rick was nowhere in sight. I went outside to comfort him on this hideous accident, but he was driving out of the garage and yelled out to me that he'd just see me at the office when I was done. "Done what?!" I yelled back. That was Rick. He had other fish to fry, like getting back to work on a big case, and I was left to clean up the mess at the house.

It was noon before the final assessment was made on the damage. The hardwood floors, wallboards, granite topped island, kitchen cabinets and counter tops would all need to be torn out and replaced. The only flooring that survived was the marble foyer. My head was spinning as I listened to the schedule of drying out, tearing down, and rebuilding. I realized that Rick wouldn't have a place to stay for a very long time. And where was I going to put all of his furnishings during the reconstruction?

When I made it back to my desk, Rick was, as usual, on his cell phone. He was laughing and telling his caller about "the look on Jude's face." I wanted to strangle him. I already was stressed over hiring yet one more paralegal (Sheri had left to go back to a previous law firm several months before), and setting up a meeting with bank auditors to go over Rick's financial statement. Now I had to add this assignment to my already overbooked schedule! "When you have the time and maybe some interest, I'll fill you in on what's going on at YOUR house!" I yelled across the hall to Rick. He told his caller that he'd call him back, put down his cell phone, and walked over to my doorway. "Man! That was a lot of water! What happened?" he asked in a tone that got under my skin. "Did a water line break or something?" "Your icemaker hose came loose from the refrigerator and has been spitting water on the back wall for at least a week," I reported in a clipped tone. "No one noticed it before now since the house has been vacant while you've been out of town." "Damn! Really?! Wow!" was his only response. He turned to walk back to his office. "Have any plans for tonight?" I asked innocently. "I don't know, Jude. What do you have in mind?!" he said chuckling. "You can't stay at the house and we have to move out all of your furniture. Got any suggestions?" "I'll just stay here for tonight (he'd had a small bedroom and shower installed upstairs when he took possession of Chesley House), and we can get my stuff moved into my Sixth Avenue house," he said nonchalantly. This is what fascinated me about the man. He never flinched. Just on to the next thing.

Unfortunately, before we could utilize Rick's plan, the universe had one more joke to play. I went to Sixth Avenue to unlock the door so our runner could come by with some provisions to keep Rick going for at least a few days. When I went inside, the place smelled of mildew. I walked through the dining room and switched on the hall light. It was "déjà vu all over again!" The entire hallway was full of water! The wallboards were stained and the oak floors in the master bedroom, guest bedrooms, and formal living room were all wet! I heard the source of the problem. A toilet in one of the guest bathrooms was running. I sloshed through the water and into the suspect bathroom, took the back off the toilet and saw the lever was stuck and a crack was in the porcelain. I grabbed my cell phone from my purse in the kitchen and speed dialed the plumber we used on all of Rick's properties. He came right over and fixed the broken toilet within an hour. Now I was left to mitigate one more house! How could this happen? Rick hadn't been here for months. Whoever was the last to use the bathroom must have left without hearing the commotion from the toilet.

Rick was gone when I finally made it back to the office around 5:00 p.m. The runner told me he had left an hour before my return and had gone to the Hotel Duval to have drinks with someone. I drove over to the hotel just two blocks from our office and found him holding court with several friends at the sky top bar. After I shared the gory details of Sixth Avenue with him, he called over the bartender and told him to give me whatever I wanted to drink. "Well, I guess I'll just stay here tonight!" he said chippily. "This place just opened and looks pretty nice. Can you see if they have a room available?" I put down my wine glass and went to find the registration desk downstairs. Within moments, Rick was ensconced in a beautiful suite with cheerful young valets attending to his every wish. "I could get used to this!" he declared. "Don't!" I barked. "We can't afford it!"

Once again, the luck of Rick Bateman held. When I had submitted the insurance claim for Millstone, the adjuster told me that Rick could stay in any rental property of his choosing and the cost would be borne by the insurance company. So, he figured he'd stay at Sixth Avenue, which wasn't his primary residence, and rent it to himself. That would have been a fun enterprise, but of course fate stepped in and scotched that dubious plan. I arranged for his stay at the Hotel Duval to be extended for a month, with all payments coming from the insurance company. Rick was in hog heaven! He acted like Conrad Hilton as he walked through the halls of the hotel in his hotel bathrobe and slippers, calling out to staff by their first names, and inviting friends to "Come on over and have a drink with me," in the palatial bar upstairs. The entire hotel was at his beck and call and he loved it. I swear he referred to it as "my hotel" on more than one occasion!

Sadly, all good things must come to an end, and when the day came for Rick to vacate the hotel suite, he was really down in the mouth. "Can't they find something else wrong at Millstone?" he whined. "Get a grip!" I shot back.

# Chapter 6

## *The Gracious Host*

Rick never went back to Millstone. He had stopped making payments on the mortgage and the bank began foreclosure proceedings on the property. He moved into his Sixth Avenue house, which had been fitted with new wood floors and fresh paint throughout, courtesy of his home insurance payout for the toilet leak. It was registered as his homestead property, and became headquarters for late night work sessions, and his favorite pastime of holding crab and shrimp boils on his large, open lawn.

He was always a gracious host and would spare no expense in giving his guests a good time, even when money was very thin. His favorite time of year was early fall when he'd dispatch our runner to St. Marks and Panacea to collect shrimp, crab, fish, and oysters for Cajun style boilin'. He'd leave the office early to fire up the fish cookers and grills and to ice down all the beer and sodas. There was no set list of invitees. He'd just start calling friends and associates and tell them to "Come on!" and they would. Loud music, mostly country, would be playing, the doors to the house would be propped open, long tables would be draped and set up on one side of the yard to hold utensils and side dishes, and folding chairs and hammocks were strewn throughout the area for anyone's use. People milled throughout the house and out on the lawn, while a select few would be with Rick as his cooking assistants in the covered breezeway connecting the house to the separate enclosed garage. The few events that my husband and I attended were still going strong when we'd leave around 10:00 p.m. The festivities never ended until the last person went home, or when Rick retreated to his bedroom to enjoy some "party favors" with his date or somebody else's!

One close friend and fellow attorney tells his own cautionary tale of partying hearty with Rick:

> *So, we show up after work, I think it was a Thursday night, with all intentions of eating some food, having some drinks, and enjoying our time with Rick and the others. I had a court appearance the next morning, so I told my wife that we really did have to leave at a decent time. Anyway, one thing led to another, and Rick was in his prime telling stories, feeling up some young lady that was there (I have no idea if she was his date or someone else's), and pushing everyone to eat and drink to excess. I'm sorry to say I was one of those who did just that.*

> *The next thing I remembered was waking up, opening my eyes that felt like they were full of sand, and rolling over to find Rick Bateman next to me! I was in his bed, naked! He was sitting up and typing away on his laptop, his glasses on his nose, and naked as a jaybird! "Good morning, sunshine!" he said laughing at*

*me. I know I must have had an expression on my face that was priceless and Rick was not going to cut me any slack in giving me the story of how I ended up naked in his bed. I stumbled out of bed, head spinning, found my pants on the floor, put them on, and weaved down the hallway hoping to find my car keys somewhere. The whole episode ended with Rick yelling to me that my keys were on the kitchen table, coffee was there also, and that my wife had hitched a ride home with someone.*

*I did make it to court somehow, but that day will go down as one of the sickest, saddest days of my life. Rick called me later and told me that he had just won the day on one of his cases. That's what really got me about the guy...he had the constitution of an elephant! I know he had to have drunk as much as I did the night before, but he was fresh as a daisy that morning!*

Halloween was a favorite party time as well. Rick loved children and delighted in seeing their costumes and going trick or treating with them. His neighborhood was family friendly, and almost every house was decorated with ghosts and goblins and lots of candy awaited the sugar craving revelers at each door. Many of Rick's friends lived in suburban areas that didn't celebrate the holiday with gusto, so he used his house as a staging area for them and their little ones to begin the evening's festivities. Parents would arrive at his house on Sixth Avenue with their children in tow. He'd always have some crazy mask on and the kids just loved it! As the parents stayed behind to hand out candy on his behalf, Rick would load up his guests' children in his golf cart and drive up and down the streets with them until all the children had at least one sweep of the neighborhood. Then, everyone would go inside and empty out their candy on the family room floor and sort through it, trading pieces of favorites and giving Rick his percentage as payment for the rides! The parents would have drinks while the children watched movies on the big leather couches and fell asleep.

One favorite film of some of the older children was an Austin Powers movie, starring Mike Meyers as the lead characters. The character of Fat Bastard, a big, fat, nasty spy who was enlisted by Doctor Evil to steal Austin Powers' mojo in a vial, brought the most laughs. One of the mothers in attendance would imitate the voice of the Fat Bastard to perfection and make everyone in the room howl with laughter. Months later, Rick asked her to meet him at a local bar for happy hour:

> *My husband and I waited for the always late Rick to arrive. Finally, he pulled up in his black Porsche convertible, ran to our table, and announced that he had the perfect present for me. He placed a Spencer's Gifts bag on the table, reached in, and pulled out a Fat Bastard plush doll. When you poked the doll in the stomach it would say, "I have a clip-on dick that would choke a donkey!" I said, "You saw this and thought of me?!" He wept with laughter every*

*time someone poked the thing. We had a great time.*

*My toddler daughter took it the next day, hugged it and slept with it for years. I was disgusted, but she just loved how big and fat it was. I regret now that we got rid of it a few years ago, especially now that Rick is gone, because it reminded us of him and all the fun times we had together.*

Rick's volatile temper sometimes made it difficult to be his friend. He had a big heart, but he could go zero to ninety in a flash - from laughing to crying, from love to hate, from who's on the list and who's not on the list. Anything could set him off, and whoever was in his sights would be the target of whatever he was feeling. He did have a few close women friends who were not lovers, which is probably why they were good friends! But, he preferred the gruffer, slap on the back kinship of men friends and often used the free and easy atmosphere of his parties at Sixth Avenue to vent his feelings on whatever was on his mind. One good friend, who often found himself one of the last to leave, shared some confidences:

*He loved having people over to his house and feeding them. After everyone left we'd get into some things. He'd say, "I don't have a lot of really close friends, but the ones I do have know that I'd do anything for them. And, I know the few friends I have would do the same for me."*

*We both got a big slap in the face after the real estate bubble burst and we both had to revamp ourselves. We saw a lot of the people we thought were friends walking away. So, you either cry or try to blow the doors off all over again.*

*After Rick died, I was diagnosed with throat cancer and had to go to Shands Hospital in Gainesville for some extensive treatment. It hurt me that not one of my so called friends came to see me. If Rick had been alive, he would have set up shop next to my bed and made passes at all the nurses while I was recovering.*

# Chapter 7

## *The Pirate and the Cowboy*

Over time, I learned that it was useless to try and figure out Rick's motives for doing some of the things he did. With that in mind, I dutifully followed his order to retrieve the original of his Will and funeral arrangements from the vault for his review. He came into my office, pulled up a chair in front of my desk, and began reading the documents. As he read through his Will, I glanced down at the piece of paper titled, "FLB Funeral Service." The two lines describing the kind of service he wanted simply said, "Celebration of Life. No sadness of dying." There was no minister requested to conduct the proceedings. Three names were listed as speakers: Paul Harden, Jude Burk, and John Morgan. One song was chosen: "Always on My Mind."

Rick looked up over his glasses and smiled, "What do you think?" "I think this is probably a rough draft that you threw together some night while you were in a silly mood." "Why? Don't you want to speak at my funeral?" "Mr. Bateman, I would be honored to speak at your funeral if I somehow outlive you. Although, I'm sure my name will slip off whenever you are in one of your moods and think I'm an old witch trying to ruin your party, like I know you do sometimes." "Jude, I have never thought of you as a witch!" he cackled. "Anyway, the song choice is really stupid," I shot back at his pointed joke. "What are you talking about?!" "It's a bullshit song! Always on my mind, really! If someone is always on your mind, why aren't you doing something about it? It's just a stupid chauvinistic song that's intended to make men feel like they're saying something romantic, when in fact they're just shunning commitment!" "So, what's your real opinion?" he mused. "What song do you think I should have?" "Oh, I don't know...the Eagles singing 'Take It to the Limit,' or Jimmy Buffet singing 'Last Mango in Paris'..." "Are you crazy?! Last Mango in Paris?!" "Well, excuse me if I think of you more as a swashbuckling pirate taking on the world than a dried up old cowboy lamenting how much he coulda, woulda, shoulda!" I shouted back at him.

I had gone too far. The look on his face said it all. It was one thing to criticize the venue, the speakers, or anything else for that matter. But, I had committed the ultimate sin...I had besmirched Willie Nelson, his favorite singer! Rick stood up, threw the papers on my desk, asked me to put them back in the vault, and walked out of my office into his and closed the door. "Baby!" I said mockingly under my breath. I was rewarded for my transgression with the blaring of Willie Nelson's entire catalogue in Rick's office for the next few days. It's not that I don't like and enjoy Nelson - I do. But that particular song has always annoyed me as an ultimate cop out for men. Boy, would I feel differently about it in the end.

As it turned out, John Morgan was deleted from the speakers list and Lee Barrett, one of Rick's and Donna's friends from Orlando, was substituted just two days before Rick's funeral. In the months leading up to Rick's death, he and John had exchanged some heated and pointed words over Rick's bad behavior at a company dinner and John's suspicion that he was doing drugs. Rick had obviously told his side of the story to his Georgia family, most likely denying everything and acting insulted. As the family had always done when wronged by an outsider (albeit, John had known the family since his youth), they circled the wagons and asked me to eliminate John from the list.

A contingent of Morgan & Morgan lawyers and paralegals attended Rick's funeral. John was not among them. He never knew that he was even on the speakers list until I told him so when I interviewed him for this book. I confided that I knew some of the back stories between him and Rick and how sorry I was for them. "So much lost potential," he said sadly.

The fact that Rick made regular reviews of his Will did not portend any premonitions of death as far as I'm concerned. Although he was a borderline hypochondriac, keeping updated copies of all of his medical records on a flash drive in his desk drawer, I think the habitual reassessment of who would receive his worldly possessions after his death was dictated by romantic shifts. There was no question that his daughters would always be the first to be designated by their father. But, later in life when he was beginning to feel his mortality and revisit past relationships, he may have felt compelled to consider including others who had meant the most to him.

I'm not sure if Rick consciously chose not to understand his financial demise as a form of blissful denial, or if he did know and felt that if he just worked hard everything would magically sort itself out. Either way, the fact that he imagined he would have a bountiful legacy to leave his chosen ones speaks volumes as to his continued self image as a wealthy land baron. And, why not? He was referred to as a "deal maker" in a magazine interview, a "gunslinger" in several newspapers covering trials in which he was shooting down the opposition, and a "magic touch" in reviews of government meetings in which he obtained huge rewards for clients like Costco, Waste Management, WalMart, and McDonald's.

Whatever his economic status, he was adamant about ensuring the financial futures of his children. He established the Bateman Daughters Irrevocable Trust (BDIT) to provide for the health, benefit, and welfare of his daughters through funding of their education, medical costs, vacations, clothing and other expenses. A group of trusted friends and relatives were selected to serve as the uncompensated Board of Trustees.

> *We reviewed random stuff, like what should and shouldn't be included for the girls' expenses, what should be divided up for college expenses, and so on. He and Donna disagreed on some items, so the trustees worked those out. I really admired Rick for setting it up. Lots of guys were making lots of money in real estate, but not doing anything like that. Rick knew instinctively that the bottom could drop out at anytime and he wanted to be sure there was something set aside for his daughters.*

From the start, Rick took control of investments for the trust and the management of its assets. Many of the trustees considered his choice of investments risky, although one purchase yielded a heftier return than anyone had imagined it would, as one trustee admitted:

> *My family had a place at St. Teresa and Rick decided to buy a house there for $300,000. This was way before the market was trending upward and we were aghast, thinking he was crazy to be spending so much! It became an investment for the girls' trust and we later sold it for $1.3 million!*

The office building on Park Avenue, that Rick had bought and then transferred ownership to BDIT, was the location of Bateman Harden for several years. The lease for the space came through another corporation set up by Rick. After awhile, the law firm's monthly rent payments became past-due and attempts to determine when they would be made were met with verbal assaults and stand offs. Eventually, the trustees hired a management company to take over the leasing of offices and collection of rents to introduce a third party to deal with Rick and his back payments issue. For some trustees, it had become increasingly challenging to continue serving in a responsible fiduciary capacity. When questioned about some of his investment decisions, Rick would bombard them with e-mails demanding that they just trust him and back off of questioning his motives. Everyone was being dragged through a messy situation that damaged relationships between Rick and family members as well as some very close friends and business associates. Some resigned, choosing to salvage their friendship with him and turn over their trustee roles to others.

*What strained our relationship was that Rick left me to make my own decisions on the trust. Rick had made a bunch of bad investments and he was trying to tell me that they were great and the trust should buy them from him. I don't care how good a friend you were, he didn't give money away.*

Pirate Rick charted his way through life and cut a large swath across the high seas of finance, only to lose it all to creditors in the end. His adventures could be summed up in the lines of a Canadian pirate song:[2]

*"Well, I used to be a farmer and I made a living fine. I had a little stretch of land along the C. P. line. But times got tough, and though I tried, the money wasn't there. The bankers came and took my land and told me, 'Fair is fair.'"*

---

[2] The Arrogant Worms, *"The Last Saskatchewan Pirate"*

# Chapter 8

## *Somewhere Past Dark Thirty*[3]

What makes a legend? Bar stories! If I've learned anything at all about Rick Bateman, it's that he loved to drink, tell stories, and get into bar brawls. I'm sure it was his form of release from all the stress and anxiety in his personal and professional lives, and his childhood rough housing certainly fed the need to get blood on himself from time to time. The main reason for his prowling bars was that Rick didn't like being alone. Most days, he would leave the office and either go somewhere for drinks before heading home, or make a date to meet at his house for some "toddies" and recreation. When he did go bar hopping, he was always the guy who women couldn't resist. As the song goes, *"Boys say, 'When's he gonna give us some room?' But girls say, 'God, I hope he comes back soon!'"*[4]

Since I separated my life from Rick's when it came to his party boy ways, I have no first hand stories. His friends have offered up some of their favorites:

> *One night we were at Main Street Lounge in Gainesville. Dan Barnett, Cellar Door Concerts,*

---

[3] Jimmy Buffet, *"Last Mango in Paris"*, Last Mango in Paris album

[4] Roseanne Cash, *"Seven Year Ache"*, Seven Year Ache album

*owned the nightclubs where all the up and coming talent came, like Tom Petty and Robin Williams. Dan and Rick became good friends. It was the first semester of law school and we had just finished our last exam, which was a big deal. About 20 law students decided to go out and we were partying all night long. Rick was at a table with some girls when some cowboys came in. One of the cowboys bumped Rick and he said, "Watch it, partner!" At that, the cowboy took a swing at Rick. Rick moved away and the punch hit one of the girls.*

*Rick jumped up and took off after the cowboy and yelled out while running, "This guy just knocked that girl out...let's get him!" I got up and ran outside with Rick. We turned around and no one from the bar was there but us. The cowboys were now circling around us and Rick had his fists up ready to do bloody battle. About this time, the club bouncer, a big, burly guy, yelled out to the cowboys that they needed to leave or else he'd call the cops. They shuffled off to their trucks, spitting on the ground as they sped away. Rick turned to me and said, "You're the only one with the balls to follow me into a fight," and put his arm around my neck. That night we became best friends and got into a lot of fights in bars over the years.*

~~~~~

*Rick and I were about the same age, ran in a lot of the same circles, but the first true meeting we had was when a young man in Apalachicola who was in real estate called me up. "Can you help me?" he says. "A couple guys are back dooring me on a couple deals and they've got this lawyer who's giving me hell." "Who is it?" I asked. "Rick Bateman," he said. I called Rick and said, "This is CW," and he said, "I know who you are." Next thing you know we were screaming at each other on the phone. I said, "Come on, Rick. This is a young guy, he's just starting out and needs you to let him have this one," He said, "You don't know what the fuck you're talking about," and I said, "Well, the next time we meet I'll show you what it's all about!"*

*About a week later, we were both in a bar somewhere. I walked up to him all puffed up and he bought me a drink, I bought him one, and we laughed about it. This was about twelve years ago. We had a similar alpha male personality and became best friends.*

~~~~~

*We were in Bailey's Bar in Winter Park one night. I was with my wife and Rick was with his girlfriend, Laura. We were having a great time. I was with a few guys at a table sharing legal conquests of the day. My wife was surveying the place and ordering drinks for herself that she directed the barkeep to put on Rick's tab, prompting him later to grumble to me that, "I'm not even screwing her, but paying for her drinks!" Lots of laughter was coming from the end of the bar where Rick was entertaining Laura and a crowd of a dozen barflies with a wild story of a recent victory in the courtroom. I got up from my table and went over to listen. When he was finished, I said in astonishment, "Rick, that's my story! I told it to you just last week!" Not missing a beat, he picked up his beer and declared, "Yeah, but I tell it better!" More laughter from the crowd. He was right. He did tell it better, as he did just about everything else better than I.*

~~~~~

*I got a job at Rosie O'Grady's at Church Street Station. After I'd been there a few weeks, Rick came to work there too. We were employed as bartenders/bouncers. Rick had a scam going with the ticket takers and made some extra money on the side.*

*There was a local rule that no drinking of alcohol was allowed on the street after 2:00 a.m. One night, a group of people decided to ignore the rule and tried to sneak out of Rosie's with their drinks under their jackets. I went over to tell them they couldn't leave the place with the drinks and one of the guys shoved me. I called Rick over and told him we needed to get the guy's license number. I turned away for a second and the same guy hit me and broke my lip with a huge ring he was wearing. I came back at him and knocked him out. I looked over at Rick and he had another one by his hair. Another guy came at me and their girlfriends were hitting us with their purses. By now, the police arrived. The fight had tumbled out into the parking lot and at that point we had no authority to fight with or retain anyone. The police were acting like they were going to arrest Rick and me along with the others, but one of them liked our moxie and let us go. The bar owner was going to fire us, but Rick argued our case and we kept our jobs.*

~~~~~

*The one thing about Rick was that you were either on his side or you weren't. If you were, he was with you one hundred percent. One time he called me and asked me what I was doing. I told him nothing and he told me to come on down to Alligator Point because he was fixing to get into a fight with a big mouth. Some guy had been showing his butt and Rick got irritated. The guy had some friends and Rick called me for some*

79

*backup. By the time I got there, he had already hit him. "He wasn't looking, so I nailed him," Rick cackled. We ended up dying laughing over drinks and he reminisced the story many times.*

~~~~~

*Rick called me at my office one day to ask me to have drinks with him. It was a commission meeting night, so I agreed to meet him after the meeting adjourned. His house had been flooded and he was staying at the Hotel Duval. He told me to meet him upstairs at the Level 8 Bar. I texted him when I got to the hotel around 11:00 p.m. and went to the bar and ordered a drink. I looked over at the elevator when I heard his voice and there he was in his robe and slippers! There were probably twenty-five people or so up there. Everyone who walked by knew him and he knew their names. I asked him about it and he said, "I come up here all the time like this. This is my home now." I thought he was the most eccentric man I'd ever met.*

~~~~~

*So, Rick calls me one day and says, "Let's go have a cocktail." It was around 4:30 p.m. and I had other things I needed to do, but thought what the heck. I picked him up and we went to Bonefish Grill. We're not there five minutes and*

*Rick has gone missing. I looked around and see him on the other side of the bar talking to a couple girls. Typical Rick. I was amused when he came back beside me and said that he wanted to go someplace else.*

*We ended up going to Café Cabernet. We walked in and there were maybe one or two other guys standing around and twenty sorority girls at the end of the bar. So here we are with this group of twenty-two-year-olds and Rick is holding court with all of them in the palm of his hand. Of course, he's buying all the drinks (I think our tab was in excess of $800) and dancing around on the bar. Rick was really putting on a show and had me married off to five of them, saying, "This is the greatest guy in the world and I'm going to let you have him and I'll take the leftovers." Around 8:00 p.m., the owner came over to me and said, "This is the third time I've had to tell you, if you can't get him off the bar, I'll have to call TPD." Around 8:30, we called a cab. Rick got in the cab and I got in my truck and went home.*

~~~~~

*I agreed to meet Rick at the Governors Club for drinks around 6:00 p.m. to discuss a case that he thought I should take. Rick was always referring cases that he didn't think he could handle with his schedule or one that was out of his field of practice, so I was grateful for the opportunity. I got to the Club around 6:05 p.m. and Rick was nowhere to be found. I asked the bartender if he'd seen Rick and he said that Mr. Bateman hadn't been in since he came to work around 5:00 p.m. I waited around ten minutes and when Rick didn't show, I texted him to see where he was. No answer in thirty minutes. I decided to fold my tent and go home.*

*Around 9:00 p.m. I got a phone call from Rick, who sounded very drunk. "Where are you?" I asked. "I don't know." "What do you mean you don't know?" "I'm somewhere dark that stinks and I think my car's dead." "Rick, if you don't tell me where you are, how can I help you?" He had hung up without even saying goodbye, kiss my ass, whatever. At this point, I didn't know what to do. I thought of calling the police, but what would they do since I didn't know where he was?*

*Next morning, Rick calls me around 7:00 a.m. sounding chipper and asks if I want to meet for coffee. We met and I asked him what the hell happened the night before. Turns out, he met someone as he was leaving his office and forgot all about our meeting at the Club. They went somewhere, had lots of drinks, did the dirty, and then he blacked out. He woke up in his driveway in the girl's car with his trash can overturned where he had obviously run into it. I didn't ask any other questions because I really didn't want to know anything else. Rick gave me the rundown on the case he was referring, we hugged, left each other to go our separate ways, and that was that.*

~~~~~

*It had been a long day and I was spent. I decided on the way home to stop by Finnegan's, a favorite watering hole in Tallahassee. I'd only been there for thirty minutes or so when Rick showed up. He had obviously come straight to the bar from a day of bird hunting at Woodbine. He was wearing his full camouflage outfit. He was already drunk and had a lady friend with him who was equally so. All of a sudden, he started dancing to whatever music was playing and then slurred, "Wait a minute!" He felt inside his jacket and pulled out two dead birds from his pocket, heads dangling. He shuffled over to the bar, slammed the birds down, and kept on dancing. It was probably the funniest thing I've ever seen in a bar!*

# Chapter 9

## *My Friend, Pablo*

Rick loved travel, especially to the Caribbean Islands and Central America. The fishing and hunting at these locales was second to none, and he would spend so many hours in the sun it would send his melanin into overdrive, yielding a rich honey tan on his face and body. We would joke to each other: Me – "You know I'm happy when I'm fat!" Rick – "You know I'm happy when I'm fat and TAN!"

The Caymans provides the kind of lifestyle and fun that play out in Jimmy Buffet songs...boat drinks, warm breezes, bare feet, steel drum music, open air bars, and girls on the half shell. Sign Rick up! He visited Grand Cayman frequently. So much so that he established a bank account at Butterfield Bank and got a cell phone number for use while he was there. His Davidson College friend, Bryce was his point of contact there. Bryce had moved to the island and established the largest food service company in the area. He and Rick had planned several projects together, none of which panned out. As fate would have it, Bryce ended up getting arrested for money laundering and trafficking drugs. Too bad Rick wasn't alive. He would have loved going down there to help with the defense of his friend.

Pictures of his trips to Grand Cayman were everywhere in Rick's office and home. Just looking at them made him happy and he never stopped thinking that he would one day retire there and take his grandchildren boating and fishing with him. His favorite trip by far was when he took his two daughters to the island as their high school graduation gift. "If I could have made time stand still, I would have," he said wistfully.

From all appearances, Rick had always been fascinated by the drug trade. He had visited that world when he was in college. His celebrity on the football field at Davidson garnered all manner of fans and hangers on, including the "fringe element." He would buy some cheap weed on the street and sell it for profit to fellow students from his dorm room, always reserving a portion for his own pleasure. While he was at the University of Florida (UF), his opportunities to get high and get tan were plentiful.

Johnny was a UF buddy and a cocaine dealer. The irony of that was the fact that his father was a police chief in a neighboring county. Johnny never excelled in the drug trade. He gave lots of his product away and put the rest of it up his own nose. This was the 80's, and sailing over to Jamaica, loading up with drugs and coming back through St. Petersburg to traffic it was fairly easy. Rick's roommate was wary of getting too close to Johnny, since he was already working with a criminal law firm, but he did take advantage of the opportunities to sail to the islands:

> *I used to sail the boats over with Johnny for the love of sailing, but wanted nothing to do with the loading and transport of drugs. We'd stay in Jamaica and party for a week, and then I'd fly back and Johnny would sail back with his coke. Rick begged to go over on at least one trip.*

Rick eventually was included in one of the sail overs and quickly made friends with a Rasta named "Honey," who was a superb water sports enthusiast. During their "trips" on the beach together, Rick and Honey devised a plan to buy a nearby castle that a local drug dealer was constructing and turn it into a hotel from which Honey could parlay his water sports skills into profitable training sessions for eager tourists. But by week's end, Rick soberly boarded the plane back to Gainesville to finish his studies. You could say the hotel plan "went up in smoke" as Honey was forgotten and the local drug dealer died before the castle was completed.

Another UF friend was Jose, whose family were Columbian gentry in Medellin. At the age of twelve, he was kidnapped and held for ransom by local drug dealers. The family paid the ransom, but the criminals did not give up the child. Over the next five years, he was shuttled around the country while the family sought government intervention to find him. Enter Pablo Escobar. The drug kingpin, who had in his pocket most of Columbia's police and judges (and killed those that he didn't), struck a deal with the family to find Jose in return for their land on which he wanted to build his country estate. The deal was quickly made (one suspects that Escobar was behind the kidnapping from the beginning), and the young man was returned to his family. A strange friendship was borne of this episode and Jose and his family were treated to Escobar's hospitality on a frequent basis. Jose was sent to UF to study medicine and was soon hanging out with Rick Bateman. The circumstances of his years in captivity were never shared with Rick. One wonders if his kidnapping experience was the reason Jose was a lifelong teetotler, never taking a drink and never doing drugs.

Arrangements were made for Rick and a couple of college friends to visit Escobar's Hacienda Nápoles in the small town of Doradal, just outside Medellin. The estate was named after the town of Naples, Italy, where Escobar had visited and fallen in love with the place and its culture. The main gates to the estate were mounted by the Cessna plane that he first flew into the United States, loaded with cocaine (it was estimated that eighty tons of cocaine were flown into the U.S. monthly by Escobar's drug cartel). At the time of their visit, no one had ever photographed the place. One of Rick's friends had hidden a small camera in his clothing, and with automatic rifle-toting guards just feet away, snapped a photo of the entrance. The picture later appeared with credit in the *New York Times* with an accompanying story of Escobar's death at the hands of authorities who had tracked him down and shot him.

A short walk from the Spanish colonial house's front door was the private airstrip Escobar had built so he could fly planes directly to his various outposts. There were exotic animals on the grounds, including hippos and antelope, as well as a huge garage that housed dozens of collectible sports cars, and a 500-seat stadium where bullfights were held.

Rick soaked up the place. He could do anything he wanted, and did. After getting high, he enjoyed lying naked in the cool grass surrounding the big house. It looked like big, green, hairy mushrooms and provided a surface that would rival the finest tufted feather bed. He asked one of the guards about the grass's appearance and was told that it looked like that because Escobar had hired locals to hand cut the lawn on a daily basis. The image of men kneeling down in the hot sun and using scissors to cut the blades of grass into perfect mounds was incredulous to Rick. He followed up with another question as to why Escobar didn't just buy a few riding lawn mowers to use on the seven square miles of property. The answer was simple and chilling. "Pablo, in his kind generosity, provides much needed jobs for the men," the guard said smiling. Of course, it was Escobar who took whatever he wanted whenever he wanted it, including the money, land, and possessions of the very men who he now was "generously" allowing to cut his lawn.

Escobar was absent during Rick's ten day stay at Hacienda Nápoles. The drug lord was tending to his business elsewhere, but had directed some of his men to entertain Rick and his friends. The men heard that Rick liked guns and hunting. Hidden under the house's carpet were missle fireworks that the thugs would launch into the village for fun. One night, they decided to treat Rick and the others to a sky show. They took their visitors out to a ridge overlooking the homes of locals beneath. They set off a line of the homemade mortars that fired projectiles to light up the sky. The damage done below can only be imagined. One casualty of the "fireworks display", however, stood dangerously close to the group.

Among Escobar's many business enterprises was the breeding and sale of world champion Rottweilers. The dogs were exceptional and sold for $10,000 - $15,000 to a celebrity list of clients around the world. The dog breeder employed by Escobar was among the crowd that night and had brought with him one of his prize studs for the visitors to see and admire. While the mortars were firing off their loads over the village, the dog picked up one of the unexploded bombs and ran with it like a toy in his mouth. Before anything could be done, it detonated, sending parts of the dog and shards of the explosive within inches of Rick's legs.

The next morning, one of the groundskeepers was ordered to clean up the mess. He brought his little boy with him. He was holding a little birdcage with a small canary inside. Rick saw the two from his bedroom window and went outside to visit with them. He was enchanted by the little boy and his bird and spent a couple hours talking with him, playing games and singing songs together. A week after Rick came back to the states, he received word that the groundskeeper and his entire family, including the little boy with the bird, had been murdered at Escobar's direction. The man was suspected of taking something from the estate (no one knew what it was), and the murders were Escobar's warning to others to not mess with his property. Rick was enraged when he heard the news. "I'm glad I wasn't around there when that happened," he threatened. "Somebody else would have also been dead."

# Chapter 10

## *Woodbine*

*"Under all is the land."* [5]

The love and acquisition of land were as mother's milk to Rick Bateman. Walking the farmland of his youth was like passing through an energy field for him. It invigorated him to hold the dirt in his hands and feel the pulse of the Wisdom Keepers who had tended to it hundreds of years before. He spoke reverently to me of his farm and hunting grounds, and likened it to a holy experience when he stood in the middle of a field and heard the wind singing through the pine trees as a flock of doves flew by. "I never felt closer to God than when I was standing out there," he offered.

Like his grandfather Leo, Rick knew instinctively what each tract of land would yield for the purpose of farming, urban development, or hunting. Leo had bequeathed portions of his acreage to his children and grandchildren, and Rick wasted no time in supplementing his. The land holdings he amassed included several beach front homes in Florida, a shopping center in Georgia and an office building in Tallahassee that were held in trust for his daughters, and a huge cattle and quarter horse ranch in Montana that was managed by his brother, Steve. But, the property that called

---

[5] National Association of Realtors, Preamble to Realtor Code of Ethics

to him most frequently was Woodbine Plantation. It was comprised of 963 acres of prime woodlands and hunting areas in Mitchell County, Georgia, with a large house where his father lived, a small cabin where Rick stayed when he visited, a pole barn, dog kennels, and stocked ponds jumping with bream and bass. The longleaf pines were timbered every few years and the brush was burned frequently to encourage the migration of bobwhite quail. Charlie, a childhood friend, remarked about the seemingly constant burning at Woodbine:

> *I went to Woodbine with him one time when he asked me to help with some of the management up there, like helping with some of the burning. Our family farm was above Mr. Bateman's farm and I can remember since I was about five years old that it was always burning! I said to Rick as we were driving by a house down the road from his, "Whoever lives there is a fire bug!" Rick laughed and said, "That's my dad's place!" I didn't know that the plantation included his dad's house.*

Rick was by far the best bird shot in the family, but deer hunting was not his forte. The controlled discipline of waiting for a deer to appear while shivering for hours in tree stands was almost intolerable for him. He would gladly take friends and relatives on an outing, but he would either sit in the truck reading and napping or simply drive off and leave his guests stranded. One very cold morning, his good friend, Ron, was the victim of his host's impetuosity:

91

*Rick was so impatient about hunting. If he was in a duck field and nothing had happened in thirty-five or forty minutes, he'd start telling stories and want to go have a drink. One time, we were at Woodbine and were going to go deer hunting. It was so cold, around nineteen degrees. Rick took one step outside of the cabin and exclaimed, "God damn, it's as cold as Donna Bateman's heart out there!" I had come prepared with all my cold weather clothing, including a face mask so I wouldn't freeze while sitting in a deer stand at dawn.*

*The night before we were going out, I had laid out my clothes on one of the leather couches in front of the fireplace. Unfortunately, Old Joe, Rick's favorite dog, had used my clothes as his bed. In the morning, Joe came walking into the kitchen with my mask stuck like Velcro to his balls! Rick got the biggest kick out of that and said he hoped it smelled good when I put it on. I told him there was no way I was going to put it on and have to smell Joe's scrotum up close and personal!*

*So, we went out and got in the truck, shivering like crazy. He put me in one deer stand and said he was going to drive down the way and get in another one. It was so damn cold, I finally did put on that mask. After about forty minutes, I'd had enough. I hadn't seen a deer and didn't hear any shots coming from Rick's direction, so I climbed down and went to look for him. I found him curled up and snoring in his warm truck.*

The only successful bagging of a deer by Rick happened literally by accident when he was a teenager. His brother, Todd, told the story:

*One night after Rick had come home from a date and gone to bed, he heard a loud screeching of tires from the highway, followed by a woman's scream. He grabbed his pistol, ran downstairs and out into the night. A local girl had hit a deer in the road while driving home, but the deer wasn't dead. Rick performed the 'coup de gras.' He had the deer head mounted and later hung it over the mantle in his cabin. Lots of great hunting stories followed about how he had bagged the big buck, but we all knew the real story!*

Many children learned their hunting skills from Rick. He would take his brother, Bert's, little boys rabbit hunting at night with a spotlight to increase their chances of shooting one. But by far, his favorite times in the hunting fields were when he had his daughters with him. He started them early, around age three, and used them as his retrievers when he would shoot down birds. The image of the two toddlers stumbling and tripping over branches as they scurried with Old Joe to find the downed birds, and scooping them up in their tiny hands, must have been a precious scene! His hunting diary was full of entries from those times:

*"Dove Hunt at Virgil's – Madison & Callie's first hunt. They learned craps from Daryl and the others and blew on dice for good luck. They picked up my birds (limit with 28 gauge). I rang the necks. Madison loved it. Callie I'm not so sure. Great day with girls!*

*Dove Hunt at Woodbine – 75 degrees, stormy with tornado watch. Most hunted, but came out of field early. Madison and I stayed until lightning threatened. Killed 10 with 28 gauge. Madison was great spotter of birds. Wonderful time spent with her. Callie chose to stay home with her mom.*

*Dove Hunt at Woodbine, Prison Ponds – 45 degrees, Daddy and me with Madison & Callie. Shot 7 ducks which Madison & Callie helped pick up.*

*Labor Day Weekend at Woodbine. Dove field behind cabin has about 600 birds. I planted sunflowers in May. Field has corn predominant with long rows of sunflowers in middle separated by peanuts. Most of corn was left since it was so dry this summer. Daddy has been mowing some corn rows. I harrowed up two passes on outside of sunflowers to spread wheat and peanuts. Key will be to hold doves until Sunday (Bert is getting married on 9/26 – opening day!) Worked Joe and Jill. Madison spent a lot of time with me and shot a 22 magnum rifle for the first time. Got tractor and jeep bogged down. Duck holes look good after hurricane rains. Callie and her mom spent most time indoors.*

*Thanksgiving at Woodbine. My favorite Thanksgiving. I spent a lot of time with Madison, Callie, and my dad. We hunted all of Butler Place, Wayne & Jolene's, and the Martins. Donna enjoyed trip. Madison and I saw a beautiful sunset. We lost 'pup' for a few hours, but he later bounded out of the woods at Wayne & Jolene's almost exactly where he disappeared."*

So great was the lure of Woodbine, that Rick would take any measure to extend his time there. Once, in the middle of a major insurance fraud case, he invited a friend and fellow lawyer to go hunting. The friend brought along one of his clients who enjoyed the outdoors. In order to keep in touch with all pleadings that were being filed and reviewing drafts of responses, Rick had a new fax machine installed at his cabin. At the time, only land line telephone communication was available in the remote location, so a fax machine provided the opportunity to read printed documents. Transmissions would print continuously onto a roll of thermal paper until someone retrieved a transmittal and cut off the printed section.

The friend's client found out about the machine and asked if he could have some important records sent to him. What followed was to be known as "The Great Fax War", as Rick and the other man received report after report until the roll of paper was exhausted and no replacement was at hand. "Well, damn it! What am I going to do now?" Rick groused to his friend. The next day was spent on a very short, very quiet hunting excursion that yielded no game. Probably because Rick was grumbling out loud the entire morning!

From time to time, Rick would receive inquiries about his land at Woodbine and offers would be made to lease or buy some of it. I knew that Rick and his father shared the property and had formed a corporation, Frederick Leo Bateman, Inc. (FLBI), through which the income and expenses for the management would flow. What I didn't know until after his death was that Freddie had not been consulted on many of the deals Rick made on selling some of the land, as well as entering into a solar lease with a company on one of the front tracts. He rarely told me anything about FLBI and kept all conversations with others about it behind closed doors. I notarized Rick's signature and communicated by e-mail with some of the buyers, but I assumed that everything was done with his dad's agreement.

Freddie was left with a broken heart after Rick died, and a tangled legal mess to clean up as a result of the secret deals. "Rick sold property and Daddy never saw a penny," Todd said sadly. "It was millions of dollars. He signed Daddy's name when Daddy was sick. It's hard to mourn someone when this kind of information comes to light. Rick set us back, but we have a lot of resilience and we're going to cut our losses and go on."

I feel certain that Rick intended to make everything right on his undisclosed transactions before anyone would have been the wiser. He was the ultimate risk taker and would roll the dice on ventures that would have others counting their losses and walking away from the table. Most of the time, his gambles paid out. But this time, death claimed him before he could play out his hand. He danced with the Devil and got tripped up as time ran out.

Rick & Steve Bateman.

Rick's high school portrait.

Rick & Laura: College sweethearts & soulmates.

*Rick & toddler daughters at Woodbine Plantation.*

*Rick & boy with bird in Medellin, Columbia.*

*Rick, Freddie, Mary Lynn, Todd, Steve, & Bert.*

*Rick & Clay Campbell at
fishing tournament.*

*Rick gator hunting at night.*

*Rick, former President Bill Clinton, & Bill Pfeiffer at
Democrat Party fundraiser hosted by John Morgan.*

*Jude & Debbie Dantin kissing Rick's photo at
his wake at Finnegan's Bar.*

# Chapter 11

## *One in Every Port*

Rick filled up a room when he walked into it. He was a charismatic, fun loving person. And, he was dangerous. He lived life in fast forward, spent money he didn't have, and fed off of romantic fantasies. Every woman should experience a dangerous man once in her life. Rick provided that opportunity to countless women in his time, most of whom still speak longingly of how they wish they could see him just once more, or worse, how they knew that they were "the only one" he truly loved.

I had a front row seat to the love life of Rick Bateman. Each new woman was the same as the last in believing that he was just misunderstood by former lovers who hadn't been able to give him the care and companionship that they offered. I liked most of them...Rick did have good taste. I screened all of Rick's calls and read all of his business and personal e-mails at his direction. It kept me up to speed on who was "in" and who was "out" at that moment in his life. I suppose he gave each woman what she needed on an individual basis, much the same way he did with clients. Whatever the woman or circumstance, he would be available and fully engaged.

He was fun in small doses, but a lot of drama came along with it. I imagine dating him was hard. Women have to take responsibility for themselves in relationships with men like Rick. Most went in with eyes wide open and seemed to really care for him. Some tried to take me into their confidence by calling me and telling me how much Rick really loved me and had said many times how he couldn't do anything without me. I would listen silently, let a pregnant pause go by, and wait for the real reason for the call...to pump me for information on what he was doing, where he was going, and if he had said anything about them. At times I felt like I was passing notes in the tenth grade! And, based on the age of some of his girlfriends, I wasn't that far off!

Although Rick was a serial lover, there were several women with whom he maintained devoted yet platonic relationships over the years. Two were fellow attorneys with whom he had worked on litigation and land deals:

> *He was a mentor to me, especially on client relations. He was my best guy friend. I was in real estate development and had a partner who wasn't making payments. So I had Rick divide up the partnership and told him I'd give him half of whatever proceeds I got. We worked great together, although there were times he could get so aggravated and then just start laughing. I hung up on him plenty of times. My jaws would literally be aching because I had been laughing so much! He was the first person I went to for advice. I still miss seeing his name on my phone when I get calls.*

~~~~

*In 2010, I'd been an attorney for a couple years and he called me and said he wanted to meet me for a drink. I had met him for lunch on occasion and he had recently referred a case to me. But, this time he sounded more serious than I remembered. We met at the Wine Loft. After ordering a drink, he said, "Listen, your marriage is not going to survive with you and your husband being attorneys. You are a rising star and you are going to outshine him and his ego won't be able to take it. So, we need to talk about that winding down and what we're going to do."*

*I thought he was going to propose a business deal, but no, he was making a marriage proposal and presenting it as a business deal! He told me I'd be an appropriate wife for him, that we got along great together and could do some really interesting cases. He said all that was out there were "drop and add" girls (college aged girls) and that was fun for a little while, but he needed someone intelligent and interesting to talk to. "I need a person I can take to events who looks good and acts appropriately." My response was, "Here's the problem. I would never let myself fall in love with you because you would cheat. Do you want to be married to someone who doesn't love* *you?" He told me he'd eventually crack me. He promised me full division of legal fees for whatever we brought into the firm, and no less than $200,000 cash a year to spend on whatever I needed. It just came out of nowhere.*

*As I drove away I was amused, but impressed with his presentation. And just recently my husband filed for divorce. He has never been supportive of me and my legal work. Rick was prescient and knew this would happen.*

Another dear friend was his massage therapist. They shared the same birthday and ran in the same social circle. She had a happy marriage and two beautiful children of whom Rick was quite fond. Her home and studio were safe harbor for him:

*He loved women and being around fun women. Those of us who knew him were taken aback by others who hated him. "How are you friends with him? So loud, so crass, he's always up and moving around. Who acts like that in public?" He does. I always wound up defending him to men, telling them that they didn't know his soft squishy inside. I never got involved in an intimate relationship with him, so I got all the good. My husband had always been generous in trusting me with Rick. He was always a perfect gentleman with me. Someone once asked him about me and Rick defended my honor and*

*never let anyone think there was anything going
on between us in light of his reputation.*

Julie Connell was perhaps his closest and most enduring
female friend. She was one of the few people with Rick at his
deathbed in Atlanta. She sat with him around the clock while
he remained on life support. She rubbed his hand and spoke
with him, only leaving his side to go to the bathroom or get a
cup of coffee. "It's funny," she told me later. "I know he was in
a coma, but whenever I'd get up his body seemed to move as
if he was agitated. I would tell him that I would be right back
and then he would stop moving."

They began their friendship when Rick's father was
purchasing land and Julie was his Realtor. She would find
suitable tracts and Freddie and Rick would go with her to see
them. She eventually became a client of Rick's when she was
included as a defendant in a lawsuit for the overcutting of
some timberland. Two men had also been named in the suit
and had their own attorneys. Rick worked his magic on the
jury and in the end, Julie was the only one of the three
defendants to be found not guilty.

The most binding tie between Rick and Julie, however,
was the creation of Southern Communities Foundation. The
foundation had been Julie's idea and she brought it to us at
Bateman Harden. The three of us sat at the conference room
table and kicked around different ideas for services to be
offered, where the first Veterans Village would be set up, and
who would be the best source for initial funding. When it
came time for a name, Julie said she didn't care what we
called it as long as the South was referenced somewhere. I
thought for a second and said, "What about Southern

Communities Foundation (SCF)?" "Perfect!" Rick and Julie said in unison. With that, the organization was born.

SCF's mission was to provide housing, health services, and employment and training for military veterans and their families. Rick is the one who insisted that families be included in the services, saying that their sacrifices were equal to the men and women who actually left home. A collection of high profile business leaders, health care providers, and financial experts were brought into the organization's Executive Committee. We applied for and received a non-profit status from the Internal Revenue Service, and aggressively sought out partners to provide sustainable "green" energy and water, affordable housing, and environmentally sound agricultural practices for the Veterans Villages. Julie and Rick traveled to Toronto to meet with one such group, and, as often happened, the trip was anything but business as usual:

> *Rick and I were traveling to Toronto on a business trip. We had been working on the Southern Communities Foundation we had created and were in the process of acquiring funding for the Veterans Village component. Rick had another business associate who thought a company in Toronto might be a good partner for providing some of the "green" utilities we wanted to showcase at the village. My husband, Chad, never blinked an eye when I told him Rick and I were going together. We stayed in the same hotel room, which Chad had*

*booked. He said that he wanted it that way so Rick could keep an eye out for me.*

*I had a stalker before Chad and I got married. He became increasingly bold in his actions, even coming inside my house while I was away and taking some of my lingerie and leaving a wedding band on my bureau. The Sheriff found his footprints all around my house outside, but he was never caught. As a result, Chad was always concerned about me being alone. He said that he always felt good when I rode off with Rick because he never worried that I would come back safe and sound.*

*So, we arrived in Toronto late in the day and took a cab from the airport to our hotel. When we got inside, we saw hundreds of women buzzing all around the place! It turned out that an Avon cosmetics convention was being held there that same week! Rick couldn't believe it and said, "Why the hell did I tell Chad I would look after you? Of all times! Now I can't meet any of these women!"*

*We went into the lounge and of course Rick was laughing and buying drinks for women all along the bar. He would occasionally come to where I was sitting to check on me for a few minutes and then go back to the others. Some of the women looked over at me and asked Rick who I was. He said, "Don't worry about her, it's business related. I promised her husband I'd take care of her." They all looked at each other as if to say, "Yeah, right!" One by one they got up and left.*

*By now it was around 11:00 p.m., so Rick groused, "Ah, geez! Let's just go up to bed!" We went up to our room. I used the bathroom first and took a long shower. When I came out, he was gone. I got into my bed and fell asleep immediately. He told me the next morning that he'd gone for a long run because of his frustration at the bar!*

Julie lost more than a dear friend when Rick died. She also lost the visionary who had made SCF a reality. The week after the fateful trip to Atlanta, he was to have met in Orlando with the initial funders to complete the contract for the first Veterans Village start up. When word reached them that Rick had died, they pulled out. The dream lives on, but Julie has been unable to find another attorney with the insight and negotiating skills that Rick had. "We are moving forward and we will see the first village in operation soon," she said. "And when the opening day comes, we will name the first facility after Rick. I owe him that and so much more. He told me when we started the foundation that he was going to ride my coattails to heaven. I guess it's the other way around now."

And then there was Laura, the soul mate he had let go in his college days. They had maintained a close friendship even after both had gone their separate ways and married others. When her husband died of cancer, leaving her with medical bills and two children to raise on her own, Rick was the first one to offer help. "It was hard, but I was determined to do everything on my own," she confided. "But, the love and emotional support Rick gave me during that time was priceless." When Rick was working with Morgan & Morgan, they would go out to dinner in Orlando, where Laura maintained her family home. She noticed a sadness in him the last few times they were together and was scared for what the future held:

> *He called me the week before he died and I met him at his apartment. He was all over the map. We'd ride around Winter Park in his Mercedes and he'd say, "I'm dating someone and don't want to look like I'm running around. Just hold my hand." And the next minute he'd say, "Why don't we get back together...circle back around." He wanted me to look at some listings that he thought he might buy for us to live in together. He was running me ragged looking at million dollar homes.*

> *I thought of him as a best friend. He had dated one of my dear friends and she was a good influence, but he couldn't be true to her. He looked so sick and I told him, "You are a train wreck. Whatever you're doing, you need to stop." He shot back with, "If you'd married me I*

*wouldn't be in this situation." He went to see my mom and put on a show for her.*

*He asked me to go to Atlanta that final weekend. I told him I couldn't because it would put us in a situation that we would both regret. We had breakfast together before he left. I knew it would be the last time I would see him.*

Rick never met a woman he didn't love, and the feeling seemed to be mutual. A close relative observed the attraction was common to the family's male issue: "Women, dogs and children all love Bateman men!" He wasn't shy with women, even if one happened to be on a date at the time of their meeting. If he'd spot one he liked in a bar, he'd go over and introduce himself, shake the lady's hand and then her date's, and plop right down next to the woman and start up a conversation with her. I'm sure many men were left wondering, "Who was that masked man?!"

It was amazing to watch a man in his fifties dating so many women of such diverse backgrounds. Rick was an equal opportunity lover, enjoying nubile young girls in their twenties one week and moving on to robust forty-year-olds the next. He enjoyed women of all races and creeds and thought nothing of savoring several of them at the same time, as an old friend revealed:

*Rick did love women! One time while we were at the lodge, he had made plans with a girl to come over for the night. Next thing I know, he's on the phone and I hear him say, "Well hell,*

111

*come on then!" So he ended up having two girls coming over that night. Coincidentally, he had also invited a lawyer and his young son to come over. It was a little awkward over dinner. Afterward, Rick said he wasn't sleepy and would stay up to "check on things." We all said, "Goodnight,", and I went to my room and the lawyer and his boy went to theirs.*

*Next morning, I was cooking breakfast for the lawyer and his son, as well as some hunters who would be arriving that morning. About then, Rick comes out of his room in his underwear scratching himself, followed by one of the girls in her nightgown, and then the other one comes out in her tee shirt and underwear. The lawyer took his young son outside and told him to go look at the dogs. He came back inside and asked, "How many others are going to come out of there?!"*

Boasting about his conquests was standard operating procedure for Rick. I would hear him regaling someone over the phone about "this girl I met last night" and what they did together, and I'd quickly get up and shut his door. I'm not a prude by any stretch of the imagination, but there are some things that just don't leave your mind after you've heard them. I didn't want to look at Rick during a deposition or business meeting and have the images he'd painted during those conversations racing up to the front of my mind.

Second only to his appetite for sex was his near clinical attachment to his cell phone. It was omnipresent, like an appendage to his body. No matter what he was doing or where he was (including meetings in chambers with judges), he would grab his phone and just start talking without thinking a thing of it. Especially annoying was his constant "butt dialing" caused by bumping the phone in his pants pocket and prompting it to hit a button programmed to speed dial a number logged in its memory. I can't begin to count the number of times I was the chosen number that was accidentally dialed. It was infuriating to see Rick's name appear on my phone screen, pick up and yell, "Rick? Rick? RICK?!" over and over until I realized it was his derriere calling! One time, just after he returned from a trip to Cuba, his cell phone addiction and delight in sharing his lusty adventures provoked a rather tense situation with his then fiancée, Bridgette. His golfing buddy recalled the story:

> *I rarely play golf, maybe once a year. But, it was one of those days and Rick called me and said, "Let's go out." It was a typical day with Rick, my sides are hurting from laughing, just him and I. He started telling a story about him being in Cuba and it's, "You wouldn't believe the women. I have a cigar in one hand, a hundred year rum in the other, and three women in bed!" He goes on and gets really graphic and tells me about the night from "you wouldn't believe." I'm laughing and he looks down at his cell phone and sees that he had butt dialed Bridgette and she was on the phone and hearing everything he*

*was saying! This is when I knew he was a genius on his feet.*

*She was screaming at him and telling him the engagement was off! He says, "Hey, baby!" She keeps screaming and cursing at him and he said without any hesitation, "You see, that's your problem. I'm telling this story about somebody else. I'm talking about what Bob did and you hear a little piece of this and run off thinking it's me I'm talking about." I stood there and watched in amazement. She knew what he was doing, but couldn't prove it, so that was it.*

Rick was definitely an acquired taste. We had several paralegals and runners who quit as a result of his lurid behavior. One poor lady, whose husband was a Baptist minister and had only been on payroll a week, came into my office, and crying said, "Jude, I will pray for you. I just can't believe how you can work for that man and stay as calm and lady like as you do. I believe he is the Devil!" Before I could say anything, Rick glided into my office, put his arm around the woman's shoulders, and began to tell an off color joke that he just heard. The squeal startled both Rick and I! She turned on her heel and literally ran out the back door screaming. Her car did a "wheelie" in the gravel parking lot, kicking stones onto my window. "What the hell was that all about?!" he said laughing. "Nothing. Just hormones, I guess." Another day, another paralegal. It was normal.

We did have one young runner who thought Rick hung the moon. He was a college freshman, and of course, what he saw and heard from his boss would fuel any young man's fantasies. One time, he went to deliver some files to Rick for a case he was conducting out of state. Rick was in between business trips. He had arrived by limousine at the private plane hangar in Tallahassee where he would wait for the files to be delivered before boarding the private jet to New York. When the runner arrived at the agreed upon time, he opened the limo door to find Rick enthusiastically engaged in sex with a very large woman in the back seat. She had been part of the case he had just won at his last venue and rode along with him to Tallahassee. The young man didn't know what to do, so he just closed the door and waited outside the car with the files. It would be the last time he would ever proceed through a door without knocking if Rick Bateman was on the other side.

As the years went by, it became painfully apparent that Rick was mixing a noxious cocktail to maintain his virility that caused some violent behavior and ravaged his body. He had been taking HGH (human growth hormone) intravenously for many years. He ordered it from a company in California, along with the needles, and injected himself several times daily. He threw Viagra down his throat like candy, and topped it off with a Xanax or two. When he finished shooting up the last of his HGH one day, he asked me to order some for him. "No! I will not participate in your harming yourself! If you want it, you get it!" "Oh, Jude, don't be an idiot! That stuff isn't hurting me. I'm gonna live forever because of it!" "Who's being an idiot?" I confronted him.

At that, he stormed down the hall and started yelling at one of our interns. The yelling got louder and louder. I went down to see what was going on. He was manic and the intern was cowering behind his desk. Rick had thrown a legal reference book at him and was going on about how useless the intern's research had been and what piss poor work he was doing. I had a ticking time bomb in front of me that needed to be diffused quickly or this would not end well.

I braced myself and stood between Rick and the intern's desk. "I need to see you in my office for a minute, please," I said in a low, even tone. "What about?!" Rick spit in my face. Where the next words came from I can't tell you. It had to be Divine Intervention. "Don't you remember? Greg is flying in tonight and you wanted to take him to your Civic Center box for a basketball game? We need to look at the seating chart so I can set it up." "Jesus! I forgot all about that! Let's go!" He ran out and I motioned to the intern to leave the building out the front door. I knew he still had a lot of work to do on a brief for Rick, but I figured he had earned an afternoon off after what had transpired. After an hour, Rick was back to himself and humming a Willie tune at his desk.

What happened that day was not unique, I'm sorry to say. And, it didn't just take place at work. Once when Bridgette was visiting, she came into my office after she and Rick arrived together. He was already on the phone with someone about business and she took the opportunity to speak with me privately. "Jude, he's on that stuff again. I can tell because he gets mean when he is. He was fine earlier this morning, but now he's getting hostile." I told her I knew about it and asked her how long she would be in town. She said she was leaving in an hour and would be glad to get out of town while he was like that.

Laura shared a similar tale, saying that while she was visiting him in Tallahassee once, he had grabbed her arm when she was starting to leave and hurt her. "I was scared. I had never seen him like that and I prayed I was going to get out of there soon. I knew he didn't mean to hurt me, but he wasn't Rick then. He was a monster."

His use of the drugs became more frequent as the age of his dates got younger. Rick was afraid of being a middle aged man and believed that being available for sex on demand was critical to his image. We were all relieved and happy when he began dating what one of his daughters referred to as "an age appropriate" woman. My hope was that he would finally have a mature, sensually comfortable partner for whom the normal Rick would be more than enough to make her happy.

Christy was a successful businesswoman in the Orlando area. With Rick's help, she had just finalized the sale of her business and was financially very well off. She was a beautiful blonde with a young son. I could tell how fond of her Rick was by the way he spoke of her to me. I finally got to meet her when she came to Tallahassee with him on one of his "road warrior" trips back and forth between Bateman Harden and Morgan & Morgan. I liked her immediately and could sense her genuine affection for him. Rick's brother, Todd, told Rick that he needed to claim Christy for his own before it was too late. "Those other women are only after your money. Don't you want a partner?" he challenged Rick. "Oh, that woman wants forever!" Rick complained. "Well, forever ain't that long anymore," Todd warned. The relationship ended a little while later.

*I know my business savvy attracted Rick to me. The timing was really tough for our relationship because my business sale was a huge event in my life in addition to having a child at home. The buyer's financing was taking a very long time and Rick kept me grounded and was really emotionally supportive. At one point I was fed up with the delays. I wanted to tell them to forget it. I didn't want to put my life on hold while they were messing around with their business plan. Rick told me to tell them that. I did (not in the colorful terms that Rick had used) and then we closed in two days.*

*After I sold, I was ready to spend time with him, but he was never around. He was in Tallahassee or New York or wherever, and would just text me every three or four days. It was not emotionally very healthy for me. If I was going to be exclusive, I wanted to see him more often. I know he wanted the relationship. If it had been another year down the road, I would have been able to manage him better, but it was a complicated time. It was just so hard to have him grounded. His lifestyle was just to come and go as he wanted.*

John Morgan tried to give Rick some relationship advice as well. "He loved fucking and chasing pussy. He probably was never meant to be married. There were a few women who came close to the altar with him, but he'd complain that one was crazy and wanted one thing and another wanted another, and so on. I told him that all women are crazy. He just needed to pick the one with the kind of crazy he could live with and be happy." Needless to say, the advice fell on deaf ears.

There wasn't a better heart than Rick's. He was pure in intent, but was a tortured soul. He was his own worst enemy and would sabotage himself when things got good. He loved being married and the concept of family, but admitted that he had a "disease" with women. "I love to have women love me," he confessed. "You sound like a college kid in heat!" I retorted. And that was his weakness and what created a lot of his problems with his wives and lovers...the never growing up stage where he could behave like a twenty-five-year-old with no consequences. But, the sheer number of women who came in and out of Rick's door belied the notion of no consequences. What temporarily felt good would ultimately result in lost love and long, lonely nights of howling at the moon.

# Chapter 12

## *A Prose is a Prose...*

"What was that from?" Rick asked me the week after I'd quoted a poem at Clay's funeral. "Edna St. Vincent Millay's, 'The Spring and The Fall,'" I answered. "It's one of my favorites." I had used the final two sentences of the poem, substituting "Tis not love's going hurt my days, but that it went in little ways" with, "It's not Clay's going that hurts my days, but that he went in little ways." "Can you recite the whole thing to me?" Rick inquired. "Sure!" I began:

> "In the spring of the year, in the spring of the year,
> I walked the road beside my dear.
> The trees were black where the bark was wet.
> I see them yet, in the spring of the year.
> He broke me a bough of the blossoming peach
> That was out of the way and hard to reach.
>
> In the fall of the year, in the fall of the year,
> I walked the road beside my dear.
> The rooks went up with a raucous trill.
> I hear them still, in the fall of the year.
> He laughed at all I dared to praise,

*And broke my heart, in little ways.*

*Year be springing or year be falling,*
*The bark will drip and the birds be calling.*
*There's much that's fine to see and hear*
*In the spring of a year, in the fall of a year.*
*'Tis not love's going hurt my days,*
*But that it went in little ways."*

"I'm going to use that sometime," Rick sighed. "Be my guest. Just be sure to give Edna the credit!"

Rick was the epitome of a Renaissance man. He was a brilliant litigator, a skilled marksman and hunter, a natural athlete, and an aficionado of poetry and prose. He would write some whenever the mood hit him. He scribbled sentiments and thoughts on sticky notes and posted them on his computer. Some of his musings sounded strangely familiar to me. After some on-line research I found that many of them were elicited from other famous people, though Rick claimed them. But, he did know just what verse would evoke the reaction he wanted and no one seemed to doubt that his writings and thoughts were original. He made them his own.

During his courtship of Laura, he wrote many letters of love and longing. The words and phrasing reveal a self realization and a heart mature beyond his years:

*"Sometimes letters are the only way to express things that never sound right when they are spoken. I know many times I don't treat you like I want to. You have to bear the brunt of all my anger and frustration because I keep it all*

*bottled up and hidden from everyone else. I hope you understand that even in its strange way, this too is a sign of my love. When you love someone, sometimes you must overcome their shortcomings. You have done this for me a number of times and I have thanked God every time that you are that much of a person. Whatever I gain in life – millions, glory, power, fame – it will all be a failure without you."*

Nanny Boutwell (Rick's maternal grandmother) was his biggest fan and he adored her. He could do no wrong in her eyes, even when he had pushed the limits of bad behavior with his mother. He would run to Nanny and she would defend him without hesitation. Her small frame house was a favorite hangout for all the grandchildren. When Nanny's mind left her in her final years and she required the constant care of others, Rick watched sadly as his great supporter slowly drifted away from him. After she died, Rick negotiated the sale of her house and property while he was out of the country. The night before the closing, he wrote the following prose to his grandmother's memory:

*"Frail and fragile, her baggy, wrinkled skin gives evidence of her time-worn life. She sits there serene, frightened eyes occasionally flickering as attendants walk by. Her day is passed. Only a minute portion remains of her once brilliant mind.*

*She was the wonder of my youth, the*

*inspiration of my adolescence, and the saint of my maturity ~ now she doesn't even know me.*

*No more Bible stories, second ice cream cones or long, flowing letters when I am so down. No more talks, no more speeches, no why's or how's.*

*I cry when I see her every time, but the fog it never lifts, she never says my name. In life she had so much to offer, but it's a pity now that she has to live.*

*Though of God I was not too certain, I pray to Him when I need her. And every night before I sleep, I say thank you – for a beautiful person."*

I'm sure one of the many reasons why Rick Bateman was the successful attorney he became was the fact that he had the heart of a poet. He crafted arguments to present to courts that had a rhythm that drew people in and held them in his spell. No doubt he honed his gift for lyric from the study of his idol, Clarence Darrow. The legendary criminal attorney, whose life and trials have been the subject of countless plays and movies, was the one figure who Rick wanted to emulate above all others.

Darrow became renowned for moving juries and even judges to tears with his eloquence. His successful plea to save the lives of Leopold & Loeb in their murder trial for the callous slaughter of a fourteen-year-old boy was designed to soften the heart of the judge and to move public opinion away from the death sentence. In fact, his closing argument was so often referenced by the media, it would have been a *New York Times* best seller if it had been published as a stand alone work. Rick, likewise, gave many speeches in hearings and in court that would have news organs and the public alike quoting him often.

*We were together for weeks after work prepping for the case involving a police officer who had been accused of racial profiling, among other things. It's still the largest case I ever participated in. Before the actual federal trial, an ad hoc panel had been assembled in Jacksonville by the Florida Department of Law Enforcement (FDLE) to determine probable cause. Rick didn't know the police culture and he had no problem admitting it and turning to me for help. I wrote the report and Rick paraphrased it.*

*There was a full docket that day and a couple hundred people were in the hearing room, including other cops from other jurisdictions who had been accused of something. When it came to our guy's turn, Rick stood up and did all the talking. You have to understand that most of these hearings are nothing more than the cops and/or their attorneys presenting factual reports in a very dry, monotone fashion. Rick, on the other hand, treated the report as a piece of poetry and presented it like a closing argument. The entire room was spellbound by what he was saying and how he was saying it.*

*When Rick was finished, the panel chairman looked right at him and said, "Well, Mr. Bateman, I've heard your expressive presentation. In law enforcement, we often say that if it looks like a duck, walks like a duck, and quacks like a duck, it's a duck. These charges are a duck! We have no finding of fault!" Everyone in the room stood up and applauded. The media couldn't get enough and covered it, along with some excerpts of Rick's presentation, for days afterward.*

Even more so than his embracing Darrowesque prose, was Rick's embodiment of the ideal of Darrow as a fierce litigator who, in many cases, championed the cause of the underdog. "He loved folks who were disenfranchised and didn't like anyone taking advantage of them. He pictured himself as Robin Hood," said a family member. One of his clients provided this insight to the man:

*Rick was very special. He was an enormously complex person. Once, I visited him at his 'divorce house' which he rented while going through one of his divorces. On his coffee table was a large book about the Civil War and next to it was another book about the Civil Rights struggle. The irony of Rick was that he was very proud of being Southern, but he was also enormously motivated and moved by the African American freedom movement and gay rights. He made me comfortable being who I was as a gay man. His breadth of knowledge and search for truth, liberal and conservative, made it impossible to pin any label on him. I thought he was enormously bright. He had a penchant for fighting for an underdog and justice.*

A friend of Rick's stopped by the office one day, obviously upset by something. She met with Rick behind closed doors for about thirty minutes. When the door opened, he was assuring her that he'd take care of everything. I exchanged pleasantries with the woman and she left. I asked Rick what the case was. He said we didn't have a case. I questioned what he had meant when he had said that he "would take care of everything." He started telling me the story of the woman's teenage daughter who was being bullied and threatened by another girl. Evidently, the "crime" being committed by her daughter to prompt the physical and emotional attacks was her friendship with the former boyfriend of the bully. The details were frightening and I thought how glad I was to be from another generation when such things would never have been tolerated in the public schools I attended.

Rick took to his computer and pounded out a letter to the bully's parents advising that he intended to file a lawsuit against her for harassment and assault. He insisted on taking care of all the details of the situation himself. I knew he was probably thinking of his daughters and how he would be outraged if anyone ever tried to hurt either one of them, so this was him acting out on that emotion by proxy. The net result of his work was to obtain a restraining order to keep the bully at bay and a fine to cover the cost of the clothes she had torn in her attacks.

Another time, Rick helped a prostitute with a housing problem. It seemed her landlord suspected she was running her business out of her apartment and he wanted to evict her. She was sent to Rick by a friend at the County Commission who claimed her as a constituent. The morning she walked into our offices was icy cold. I was just taking off my coat at my desk when she walked up to me and announced that she had an appointment to meet "Mr. Rick." I knew nothing of the pre-arranged appointment, so I asked her to have a seat while I contacted him on his cell phone. This sort of thing was not unusual. Rick would meet friends and associates after hours and they would tell him of their own or someone else's need for legal intervention. Of course, he never bothered to warn me of any of these spur of the moment meetings! I called Rick's cell phone, but he didn't pick up. She said she could wait a little while and sat down in the side chair next to my desk.

I tried hard not to stare at her, but it was a sight that I had never seen up close and personal. Despite the freezing weather outside, she was dressed in the kind of shorts referred to as "Daisy Dukes", with black knee high stiletto boots. Her exposed stomach draped over the top of the shorts. A pink tube top was doing its best to restrain her triple D bosom. At least twelve gold bangles clinked on her arm as she moved. Black eye liner was smudged beneath her eyes in a way that looked as if a mistake had attempted to be erased, but the result was smeared blobs of kohl that clung to her pockmarked checks. The lipstick was the brightest red I'd ever seen and intensified the yellow stain of her teeth. Whatever drug store cologne she was wearing was beginning to make me nauseous.

Just about the time I was getting ready to open a window and ask her if she wanted to re-schedule her meeting, Rick came breezing in. Without slowing down, he simply motioned to her to come into his office. He closed the door. My mind was racing with all kinds of random thoughts, including some X-rated ones. The meeting lasted only five minutes. The door opened, she walked by me smiling, and left. Rick was on his phone when I went in to ask about what had just happened. "Yeah, you do that!" he yelled into the handset as he slammed it down. "Who and what was that?!" I asked. "Just a girl who works hard for her money and can't get a break," Rick mused. "Is this a case or are you just helping a 'friend'?" "What do you want it to be, Jude?" "Neither!" He let out that infuriating cackle that he used when he thought he had gotten a good one over on me. He was ready to move on to the matters at hand for the day, but I couldn't let it go. "Tell me what the heck you're doing with that woman!" I demanded. He quickly told me the story of her landlord woes, his call to the guy and the guy's angry tirade on the phone threatening to have Rick disbarred for soliciting, and his challenge to the man "to do that" I had heard when I walked in. "So, what now?" I asked. "So, now nothing. I promised a friend that I would make a phone call on her behalf and I did. End of subject."

The episode stayed in my mind all morning and I

recollected how many people in all walks of life had come through the door to have the famous Rick Bateman take their side on something. Those who presented themselves as "above reproach" and would be bombastic in their attacks on him in public, would call him for a "behind closed doors" meeting when they found themselves in need of counsel. Rick knew they were hypocrites, but he didn't hold a grudge and would agree to a meeting or phone call with these double dealers. They got the relief they sought and he never got recognition for it. I witnessed it many times. He didn't judge a case on its merits of winning or losing, or on the size of the bank account of the person, but on doing the right thing for someone. He never used the word "justice", believing in the quote from Epicurius that, "There is no such thing as justice in the abstract; it is merely a compact between men."

I found the poem by Omar Khayyam that Clarence Darrow quoted in his closing argument in the Leopold & Loeb case and had it framed, along with a sepia portrait of Darrow, and gifted them to Rick. When I handed them to him, he read the poem out loud:

> *"So I be written in the Book of Love,*
> *I do not care about that Book above.*
> *Erase my name or write it as you will,*
> *So I be written in the Book of Love."*

He took the framed poem with him to his office at Morgan & Morgan in Orlando. After he died, it was one of the few things of his that I wanted to claim for my own. But, it was not among the items cleared from his office or apartment. I like to think that maybe Rick has it with him in the spiritual world, claiming it as his own.

# Chapter 13

## *Matlock on Steroids*

"You need Rick Bateman!" Those are the words of advice that many heard when they were in need of legal representation, as numerous clients relayed to me when engaging our firm. Former clients, business associates, fellow attorneys, public officials, friends and enemies alike would recommend him without hesitation. "I was told by some people who didn't know him, but knew his reputation for being unorthodox, that I should steer clear of him," one man divulged to me. "I am so glad I ignored them and went with Rick. It was true that he was brash, rude even, but was unstoppable in his pursuit of justice for me. I think all attorneys should be like that! I never doubted that he only had my best interest in mind. No one did it better!"

What made Rick so effective was his intuitive nature that gave him the ability to morph into whatever personality was useful for each particular venue. While representing a major insurance carrier in a Worker's Compensation case, he could be the most sophisticated and debonair counsel on the planet, with only his Southern accent hinting that he was not of the New York corporate ilk. He could then go into a Dixie County courthouse in a khaki jacket and cowboy boots, shuffle papers at the small desk in front of the judge, tell long stories of vaguely applicable reference to the case at hand,

and have the entire courtroom in stitches. And in both circumstances, come out the victor while opposing counsel scratched their heads wondering what had just happened.

I called him "Matlock on steroids" as a reference to my favorite criminal defense attorney played on television by Andy Griffith. I saw him as the story telling country boy with the thick-as-Karo syrup drawl, coupled with the physically imposing Mr. T of the "A-Team" ("Pity the fool who didn't take him seriously!") I'm sure the Matlock reference would have made all the sense in the world if Rick had actually practiced criminal law. But, given the fact that he was a civil litigator where he had to argue the merits of business and government rulings, it took on a different connotation. He took the cut and dry profession of civil law practice and made it exciting. And, he did own a seersucker suit!

> *There was a pretty testy hearing and Rick was pushing the limits of what I consider respect for the bench. After the hearing I told Rick he was pushing the judge pretty hard and a lot of judges would call you up on it. Rick said, "I don't think so!" Rick had to be back in front of the judge a week or two later and told the judge that he apologized for being in any way disrespectful, saying, "My associate told me I pushed the limits." The judge said, "Well, Mr. Bateman, I didn't think you were any different than you always are."*

~~~~~

*There was a big federal case where we were representing a policeman accused of being racist. He had also taken on the union for assisting in stacking the deck against him. Rick was taking the deposition of one of the municipal officers in downtown Orlando and I was there to assist him with all of the questions and exhibits that we'd prepared for weeks. All of a sudden, he just stopped in the middle of his questions and said he needed to take an early lunch break. I didn't know what was going on, but before I could ask him he bolted out of the building.*

*About thirty minutes later he came running back in with a huge mounted article from the 80's about a City Commissioner from Broward County, I think, who was wrongfully accused of rape or something. City fired him. It later comes out he was innocent and all the stuff had been made up. Rick had remembered seeing a framed article about it in an attorney friend's office down the street and went there to get it on the break! He comes back with it and used it as a prop while he was deposing the official. He was passing this huge thing around the table and wanting it labeled as an exhibit, and saying, "You see, this guy's life was ruined by false charges, just like my client's life is being ruined by these false charges," and then asking the official if he agreed that the guy's life had been*

133

*ruined, and on and on. I was dying laughing inside and had never seen anything like it! Rick had other cases to tend to, so I ended up finishing the deposition and asking the real questions we had prepared. It sure was a dull procedure after Rick left the room!*

~~~~~

*Rick represented Humana and I represented most of the proprietary hospital systems in Florida following the collapse of the Medicare managed care company. It involved fifty or sixty lawyers in early proceedings. The case went on five or six years. I was in federal court in Tallahassee quite a bit, and meeting with Department of Insurance representatives. It was quite a cast of characters, in which Rick was prominent.*

*We were taking depositions at State Mutual offices in Worchester, Massachusetts. There was a group of lawyers who were serious litigators, while others would just attend depositions and read newspapers, play with crossword puzzles, and in essence do nothing for their clients. Rick was annoyed and didn't want to suffer because of some of those guys. So we decided to divide up some of the depositions and separate ourselves from those losers. One guy, Bill, had been a protégé of Chesterfield Smith. Bill conducted one of the best depositions I'd seen, but later had a collapse that was alcohol and cocaine induced. He just walked out on a trial that he was head of. He was found a couple weeks later in Key West, shacked up with a couple of prostitutes.*

*One thing I remember from the litigation: The judge was still sitting on the case when the state Department of Insurance commenced an independent action which they were handling very ineptly. They had a guy on their team who was a professor at the law school. He was morbidly obese, and when he sat down, the chair squeaked loudly. I said to Rick, "I bet it's the first time an inanimate object screamed out in pain!" Rick would tell that story many times.*

~~~~~

*He was a walking story. Everything he said was crazy memorable. I was assigned to assist in a case Rick brought with him to Morgan & Morgan. I went to Dixie County twice at this country courthouse. I'd drive up from Orlando and Rick would drive down from Tallahassee and we'd meet there. It was an introduction into Rick. To see him in a courtroom was eye opening to me. He was the only one I've ever seen interrupt a judge and opposing counsel, and everyone just stopped and listened to him. He could get away with things like that because of his personality. If I did it, they'd walk me out the door. I knew he owned at least a BMW and a Mercedes, but he always made it a point to drive his pickup truck to those hearings.*

~~~~~

*When the Women's World lease thing happened, I knew that I had weak legal standing. When my lease was going to expire, I was talking with Eastern Federal, who owned the strip mall, and we cut a deal verbally. They sent me a five year renewal lease, but I wasn't completely happy with it since my business wasn't doing that great at the time due to the economy. I told them I'd do a two year lease instead and they agreed. I didn't get anything to sign, so we just went on as usual with business. In two months, I got a letter telling me I had to move out. I figured we'd have to do a settlement with this big national company, and Rick was the only one I knew with balls enough to do it. Rick told me that we were not going to settle and I just had to hang with him. He died before we could get something going. It would have been fun, because I knew Rick would have come up with something that would have really tied them in knots. I remember talking with quite a few other attorneys about it after Rick died, and without exception, they all agreed that no one other than Rick could have pulled it off, so I didn't go forward with it.*

~~~~~

*I met Rick in Boca Raton around 1989, when I was an in-house lawyer at National Council on Compensation Insurance (NCCI), the nation's most experienced provider of Workers Compensation information, tools, and services. I convinced my bosses to hire Rick to handle some complex high dollar insurance fraud cases. He paved the way for this kind of litigation, and was one of the first - if not the very first - to use the Racketeer Influenced and Corrupt Organizations Act, commonly known as the RICO statute, to recover money FOR insurance companies. Rick spent countless hours unraveling these schemes, and we met often with the FBI.*

*Our first case was in federal court in Hartford, Connecticut. Lawyers from many insurance companies came to watch. They were appalled when Rick started talking to the judge in an almost folksy, very Georgia way. But he was by far the smartest lawyer in the courtroom that day and many days thereafter, and won over a very strict judge - Ellen Burns. This was one of the oldest operating federal courthouses in the country at the time and was very impressive.*

*The defendant, Joe Gall, had been the largest employer in Rhode Island. He was a big guy with only two teeth in his mouth and had many ties to the Mob. He brought his body guards to the federal courtroom with him. We decided to file the case in Connecticut instead of Rhode Island because a U.S. Attorney told us that Gall owned half of the judges and prosecutors in Rhode Island. At one of the first hearings, Gall's lead lawyer walked over to our table and said to Rick, "Mr. Gall would like a few words in private with your lady associate (me!)" I stared straight ahead - secretly quite terrified. Rick got up from his chair and burst out laughing! He said in a loud voice, directly to Gall, "Well, I bet he would! But please tell Mr. Gall that will NEVER happen!" Rick helped me learn to be fearless about litigation that day.*

*Gall and his office manager had falsely described their operations and payroll in applications for Workers' Compensation Insurance, issued falsified certificates of insurance, and collected premiums from client companies for time periods when there were no policies in force. Gall also created false financial statements in order to obtain bank loans. He claimed to have obtained coverage from Ascona, a fictitious insurance company he created. The falsified financial statements were certified by Scinto & Company, a fictitious certified public accounting firm he also created. At times Gall used the name Tom Martin, and held himself out to be an attorney.*

*When Rick was through, Gall was convicted of conspiracy, mail fraud, wire fraud, false statements, and failure to file tax returns in connection with his operation of Labor Force of America, Inc. and Employee Staffing of America, Inc. He was sentenced to 110 months of incarceration in federal prison and ordered to pay $13.7 million in restitution. He was also prosecuted for similar crimes in Massachusetts. Gall's bookkeeper hung herself.*

*This was our first multi-million dollar judgment. Rick got a limo and some champagne for us to ride around and celebrate. My boss was so pleased that she chartered a flight back to Florida for us. No one ever again questioned my wisdom about hiring the guy from Georgia.*

~~~~~

*After Hurricane Andrew and the first big wave of hurricanes in Florida, insurance companies were pulling out of the state. I was working within the Insurance Commission as manager of the state guaranteed insurance coverage entity, Joint Underwriters Association (JUA). I was the point-man to implement strategies to improve the private marketplace. The state hired Bankers Life Insurance Company to process claims. Then, the Legislature determined that we needed to go through a bid process for the claims administration work, which we proceeded to do. Bankers lost out and somehow thought I had cheated them out of the contract, even though I was only part of the selection process and didn't have the power or authority to reject any proposal on my own.*

*They hired someone to wiretap my phone, ransack my home, and take some of my personal documents. I got up one morning and went outside to get my newspaper and the FBI was there. A phone company repairman discovered the wiretap while he was on a pole in the neighborhood. He was trying to find out why poor phone reception in the area had been reported by several homeowners, and it turned out it was the wiretap that had caused it. The phone company notified the FBI. They asked me all kinds of personal questions and wanted to know if I knew someone who would want to gather information on me. I told them that I didn't.*

*The FBI traced the tap and found the guy who set it up. He was also the one who had stolen documents from my home. He said that Bankers had hired him. They wanted to "out" me about being gay and other bizarre things to extort me. I couldn't believe it and started contacting several big name lawyers who never called me back. Rick read the story about it in the newspaper and contacted me. He said he'd really like to help me if I needed a lawyer. I knew him through dealings with insurance work he had done while he was working with a receiver. I remember people saying I shouldn't go with Rick because he had a small firm and I'd be better off with a big one. But, I had one hundred percent confidence in him and I don't know if I could have continued the lawsuit without him. He made me comfortable being who I was.*

*I just fell in love with Rick. The thing about him was I always felt protected. He had such a good read of his clients. He was emotionally invested. He was the type that would look over at me during an especially tense questioning by opposing counsel and call a break so I could gather myself. He'd even hug me if he thought I needed it. He was a fighter who terrified the opposition. People who didn't know him like I did hated him, especially other lawyers.*

*Emotionally, the trial was terrible and went on for years. I still had my job, and the state was suing Bankers too, but it was a real challenge for me. Bankers' lawyers even dragged my mom into it, asking about her sex life, how my father treated me, and all manner of disgusting stuff. They wanted to show that whatever emotional breakdown I was experiencing wasn't because of what they had done to me, but maybe what I went through as a child.*

*Late in the case, Rick had to drop out. He had merged his firm with another one and they found there was a conflict with my case since the firm he had merged with had represented Bankers at one time. Rick was quite upset about it, but he found me another lawyer and gave him all his notes. We eventually settled the case in 1997, and to the end, I considered Rick my champion.*

*He was larger than life to me. He was my friend, counselor, confidante, and lawyer. I'm so grateful he was part of my life. He changed my life in a major way. Going through the Bankers lawsuit process was a real catharsis and made me better understand myself and enhanced my self respect.*

~~~~~

*I knew him from times when we had done a little bit of fishing together. There was just a connection with him and we had meaningful conversations. I used to always think that Rick was a hot head attorney, really smart. I'd talked with him about a couple small things, but I didn't know how I'd ever use him in my business dealings. Then, my son was in a horrific motorcycle accident. The next morning Rick was at the hospital. He said, "If you want me to, I'll do everything legally that has to be done so you don't have to worry about a thing, and it won't cost you a penny." It was the most personal need for a lawyer anyone could have and I knew at that moment that he was really special to me.*

~~~~~

*I didn't know Rick Bateman before he joined our group. I didn't know he was coming. Then, one day, I was coming in the office and passed an agitated figure speaking on his cell phone. His hair was unkempt and tousled. He wore a suit, but seemed to not have a care in the world as to the detail of its appearance. Although he did not know me, he tugged on my jacket and signaled for me to wait for him to finish his call.*

*When his call ended, he eagerly introduced himself. "Rick Bateman", he said, flashing a wide smile and pulling me along with him towards what turned out to be his new office.*

*He was funny. He was genuine. He told me stories in our first meeting that made me laugh. He told me stories that made it clear to me he had tried cases, and liked to try cases. Yes, he struck me as a little unpolished, even for a small town like Orlando. But, having spent a few years in Tallahassee myself, I knew that he was one of Leon County's finest.*

*I got to work with Rick. I remember one memorable time I went to Tallahassee to help him prepare for and argue a hearing on a case we planned to appeal, and it was anticipated that I would work with Rick on the matter if the appeal was successful. He squired me about Tallahassee in his 7 Series BMW in the middle of summer with the windows down, himself apparently having no need for or desire of any air conditioning or circulating air. It had to have been over 100 degrees inside his car. We went to the Legislature and met with the General Counsel for the Insurance Commissioner and then, seriatim, with a host of Attorney General representatives to discuss the underlying case. I remember his coat always buttoned, with that button threatening to break its mooring at any time and sail like a rocket into space. I remember grinning and shaking my head at the fact that no comb ever visited his head before or during our meetings. And, although I had practiced law for almost thirty years myself at the time, I remember listening in disbelief to the colorful language with which he freely peppered his conversations with these important government officials.*

*We had lunch and dinner in Tallahassee that day. Rick's table was like a mandatory stop for everyone in each respective restaurant. He knew everybody, and everybody knew him. And there were laughs, lots of laughs, on each occasion when someone stopped by.*

~~~~~

*By the time I was twenty-five, I had been working in real estate for several years and had established a branch office for a national company in Monticello, Florida. My brother was working in land clearing. One day, I was asked for a recommendation of a logger for the clearing of some land. I recommended the one who my brother was working with. Unfortunately, the land was overcut and there was some suspicion of who gave the direction to cut the extra timber and what had happened with the money for the additional cuttings. I was sued for $150,000 damages.*

*Although I had nothing to do with the hiring of the guy or any work done, I had been listed as a defendant along with two other men when the lawsuit was filed. The Plaintiff thought I had Errors & Omissions (E&O) Insurance for my real estate company, from which he could recover the money to make up the overcutting, so he included me. I didn't have E&O and Rick immediately saw that my inclusion in the lawsuit was frivolous, so he crafted a settlement agreement for me in which I offered $1 for my name to be dropped. It was refused and we went to trial. I had Rick as my attorney and the others had their own legal counsel. This was going to be a jury trial. Most of the jurors had limited educations, so it was going to be a challenge to present my case without going into too much legal rhetoric.*

*On the opening day of the trial, Rick was physically getting further and further away from the others who were being sued because he didn't want me to be associated with them. The rural courtroom wasn't all that big, so it was almost comical to watch him pick up his legal papers and move his chair further down the table. Rick had told me to wear clothes that looked bad and to not wear any makeup. That's when I realized what an amazing attorney he was – he was staging great theater.*

*Even though we had met often and I told Rick every conceivable piece of information he had asked for, I stayed up the night before the last day of the trial to write a closing argument. I felt Rick would need it for reference to the many things that had been discussed. Rick got up before the jury the next day and said, "Ms. Connell was so worried about her reputation, it means the world to her, that she stayed up all night and wrote all of these notes. This is her life and she hasn't done anything wrong." He waved the dozens of pages around in the air and then said, "I'm happy to have these and I'm going to put them right down here to check on if I need them. In the meantime, they will help steady this podium." He folded the papers and placed them under the podium and smiled over at me. I was sick! I was thinking, "What are you doing?! You're not going to use my notes?!"*

*Rick was wonderful. He not only presented a great case, he was humble and made the jury feel comfortable with what he was saying. I trusted him and he was amazing. I thought he was ignoring me when I'd told him things, but he remembered and used almost everything we'd discussed. He never referred to my written notes under the podium.*

*At the end, the jury gave their judgment on each of us. The first guy stood up and was told he was found guilty of coercion, trespassing, and theft. The next guy...guilty on all counts. Rick was breaking my hand he was holding it so hard as we stood together waiting for our verdict. I was found not guilty on all counts.*

*I had worked with Rick's dad on some land deals. That, coupled with using him for my trial attorney, brought us together as the best of friends. I adopted him as another brother.*

One case that Bateman Harden took on was personal to me. Steve Leoni, a very successful businessman, wanted to sue his Skybox licensing partners. Steve and two other business owners had come together to purchase a Skybox at Florida State University's (FSU) Doak Campbell Stadium for watching FSU home football games in lavish comfort. Each partner would contribute thousands of dollars over a period of six years to cover the cost. The Skybox also came with several premium parking spots at the stadium.

Steve and Rick had a mutual friend in Clay Campbell. Steve had hired Moore Bass Consulting for engineering and permitting work for his myriad building projects over the years. I had gotten to know him through my work there and liked him very much. The fall before he died, Clay called Steve to ask if he might use the Skybox so he could take his 4 year-old son to an FSU home game. He wanted to enjoy some father/son time with his little boy before the cancer claimed his energy and he would be unable to leave his bed. He was already getting too weak to walk any great distance, so the opportunity to drive right up to the gate and take an elevator up to the luxury box seating would make the outing much easier.

They chose the date and Steve notified his two partners of the arrangement. The partners told him all of the seats were already promised to others as well as the parking spaces. Steve was furious, especially since he rarely went to any of the games in deference to his partners' needs, but more so because he was trying to honor a dying friend's request and his partners didn't seem to care or understand that. He ended up getting seats and parking for Clay from a fellow Skybox owner, but his anger prompted him to investigate why it seemed his partners were always making excuses about the availability of the luxury stadium seating.

Rick took the case without hesitation. Clay's death was still a painful memory and he was determined to help Steve uncover whatever it was the two men were hiding. And did he ever! Not only did he convince a jury that the men had committed civil theft (not an easy thing to do), but he got Steve an award of treble damages and attorney's fees! It was one thing to convince a jury of how badly these rich men had played together, but to have them believe in the crassness of the partners' actions to the point where they literally threw the book at them, was nothing short of amazing! The press story tells the tale:

> *"On Wednesday, November 2, 2011, a Leon County jury handed down a verdict of civil theft in a case involving the purchase of a Skybox license at Florida State University. The jury found that Leoni's partners and a company they created to deposit the ill gotten funds, had*

*committed civil theft in their dealings with Leoni Properties, Inc. The verdict should result in treble damages and an award of attorney's fees to Leoni Properties, Inc.*

*The case arose out of the 2002-2003 purchase of a Skybox license at Florida State University, Bobby Bowden Field, Doak Campbell Stadium. Leoni and his two partners had agreed to purchase the box, with each contributing like amounts over a period of six years. The complaint in the case alleges that a Limited Liability Corporation was created, formed, and utilized as a sham device for the individual defendants to engage in improper, illegal and/or ulterior purposes, and to allow the defendants to convert Leoni's funds to their personal use and benefit.*

*In his closing argument, the attorney for Leoni Properties, Rick Bateman, argued that theft in a business context was no different than any other type of theft. "Stealing is stealing," no matter the circumstances, he pointed out.*

*Mr. Bateman commented after the trial that, "The truth will prevail. It always does," concluding that the best way to find out the truth is to allow our legal system to do its job, and for a jury of peers to interpret the facts as put before them."*

I attended the trial and saw firsthand the magic of Rick Bateman in a courtroom. One affectation that always had me in stitches was his wearing of reading glasses on his head. These were the kind that clicked together at the nose with magnets. They would be in two separate pieces on a cord around his neck when he entered the room. He would then nonchalantly let the magnets find one another and place the connected glasses on top of his head when he was talking. When he would get to the courtroom podium and had to look down at his reference document, he'd flip his head back and they'd come down and land in the perfect position on his nose! Ta-da!

Whenever he questioned a witness, he would walk right over to the jury box and make eye contact with the one juror who he felt was the most sympathetic to his case. I grinned when I saw juror after juror nod their heads as he was making a point. As he spoke, he would ask the court reporter if she was getting it all or if he should slow down. She assured him she was doing fine. No one seemed to mind the one-on-one dialogue. He did the same with the jurors, confessing to them that he was worried about his speech clarity since "Ms. Burk" always complained of his talking like he had marbles in his mouth. He then motioned toward me, to my great chagrin, and then looked back at the jury. Smiles all around.

I was grateful to Steve for the case, not only because of the Clay connection, but because the law firm was having a serious financial crisis. Rick was coming up on a balloon payment for the purchase of the Chesley House and we did not have money in the bank to cover it. He was also facing another hearing on his and Donna's marital settlement and his personal bank account was worse off than Bateman Harden's. Steve's fees were helping me cover payroll and operating expenses. It was, therefore, an irritant to me when Rick came over during a brief recess in the case and asked me to order lunch for everyone...our staff, Steve and his people, opposing counsel and their people, the court reporter, and the bailiff! I was thinking, *Wait a minute, buckaroo! You haven't won this case yet!* But, Rick knew what he was doing. I ordered sandwiches from the best sandwich shop, complete with sides, gourmet cookies, and a variety of drinks, and had them delivered to the courtroom. With very few exceptions, everyone ate together and thanked me repeatedly for the food. Rick enjoyed playing the perfect host, and after all, this was HIS courtroom!

After he died, I heard that countless employees in courthouses throughout the nation shed tears at the news of his demise. Rick always took the time to speak with security guards, bailiffs, judicial assistants, parking attendants, receptionists, and secretaries whenever he visited or had a case in a courthouse. For weeks after his funeral, I received messages of condolence from many of them. One courthouse guard called me, crying inconsolably, and said that Rick was the only attorney who ever asked about his family. His daughter had been raped several years before and she was now a recluse in her father's house, frequently attempting suicide. Rick stopped by the man's house one day after a trial and spent two hours with the young woman, just holding her hand and telling her that she was safe now. He always sought the guard out and asked after her.

Rick genuinely didn't think he was better than anyone else. I don't care if it was someone shining his shoes or mowing his lawn. In some ways, he was even more comfortable with those individuals who were at the lower end of the income spectrum. He didn't have to be "on" with them. With most everyone else, he felt he had to be on stage.

Law students would line up to work as interns with Rick. They would be referred to us by the director of the FSU Law School's Placement Office and I would interview them and choose one or two that I felt would fit best with our needs at the time. Rick would meet with the selected ones for a few minutes and then welcome them aboard. It was sometimes agonizing to watch the "young lions", as I referred to them, take abuse from him without knowing what exactly they did to deserve the punishment. He treated them like indentured servants and I cautioned him more than once to lighten up on his criticism. They would come to me and ask for guidance. I would tell them that they shouldn't take anything Rick said or did personally, that he was merely testing their mettle, and to use the experience as part of their on the job training. Most of them took my advice, and those who didn't parted ways with us shortly after joining the firm.

Although he provided extraordinary insights on case law when he was feeling generous, Rick was not a very good teacher. He had mastered his craft through experience, proclaiming that no one had ever gave him anything in the way of direction, and felt it was the best way for others to pick up all the nuances of civil trial law. He subscribed to the principle of Thomas Edison, who said that, "Genius is one percent inspiration and ninety-nine percent perspiration." The majority of our interns went on to receive their law degrees and pass The Florida Bar exam. I was gratified to receive a few handwritten notes from our "lawyers in training" when they obtained their first jobs in law firms throughout the state. They thanked me for helping to guide them through the form and structure of crafting pleadings. I felt it was critical to "grade" the style and composition of the filings the interns drafted. "You will be a lawyer some day and perhaps in the position to hire paralegals," I told them. "You need to know yourself what the accepted form is for each county, state, and federal court so you will be able to determine the level of knowledge and experience of those you hire." The most touching part of their notes, however, was when they confessed that they had learned more about the law "from their time spent with Mr. Bateman" than from anyone before or since. I'd share the notes with Rick, who would smugly state that he knew the writers of the notes were "the good ones" all along.

Rick never asked permission for anything. He'd just do something and if necessary, apologize after the fact. His attitude was, "If you don't try, how will you know?" A case in point: He was attending a very high profile fundraiser for the Democrat Party at John Morgan's house. John was one of the largest fundraisers in the nation for the party and had access to just about anyone in public office. Former President Bill Clinton agreed to be in attendance that night to help garner a large crowd. As such, a coterie of Secret Service agents were positioned around the property in addition to several local law enforcement officers who were handling traffic control. When Rick arrived at the event hundreds of cars were already lined along the street out front. So, not wanting to be late trying to find a parking place, he simply drove through the big gated entrance. Dozens of agents and police were screaming for him to stop, but he proceeded around the circular drive and into the open garage. When he opened the car door, he was immediately tackled to the ground by six or seven agents demanding to know who he was. "I work with John Morgan and I'm here to attend the fundraiser!" he grunted while trying to remove his head from the lock one of the men had put on it. After a few tense moments it was verified that he was not a terrorist or assassin and was let go. He ended up having to park out on the street anyway, but at least he had tried to get closer!

To this day, I get phone calls and e-mails from people looking for legal counsel. "I need a lawyer...where the hell is Rick?!" is the common message. I empathize. I lost my advocate as well. While I never intended to do anything that would cause me to need a barracuda attorney, I was always secure in the knowledge that if I ever found myself in trouble, all I would have to do would be to call Rick and say, "Help!" That's who he was and that's what he provided to all of us who knew him. And that makes me wonder: Who was his champion? When did he yell out for help and no one answered? It's a thought that haunts me still.

# Chapter 14

## *The Girl With No Arms*

Rick delighted in being around children, most likely because he had the soul of a child inside him. No matter where he was or what he was doing, if a little boy or girl was around he'd stop everything to speak or play with them. He was especially sensitive to those innocents who were challenged with special needs, which prompted his support and designation of the Special Olympics as his favorite charitable organization. He gave of his time and money to the group, including service at the local chapter of the association's state board.

Several friends of Rick's had children with varying mental and physical disorders. It was uncanny to the parents to watch their offspring, who for the most part were silent to outsiders, connect through their own telepathy with Rick. His friend, Julie tells the story of how her mentally retarded brother not only communicated, but took on observed mannerisms of his hero:

> *My oldest brother, Buddy is profoundly retarded, but is a pretty good judge of character. People who don't dote on him, he likes. Those who do, he shuns. He has limited hearing, but he always heard Rick's loud, gruff voice. I went by Rick's house one day and took*

*Buddy with me. Rick was hanging out back by the pool with a couple other guys. He introduced me to a friend who I ended up dating for years. Buddy was close in age to Rick, around 40 years old at the time. I went inside for a minute and when I looked out, Rick was picking Buddy up like a baby and putting him on a float. I froze because even though he was much shorter and lighter than Rick, I was worried that Buddy would scratch him or act out because no one, including me, had ever been able to do anything like that with him.*

*Rick popped a beer for himself and one for Buddy and then started walking around the pool pulling Buddy on the float. He just loved it! When he was ready to get out of the water, he'd let Rick know. Once again, Rick picked him up in his arms and walked over to a chaise lounge and sat him down.*

*He was so fond of Rick. Whenever I went to Rick's office and took Buddy with me, he would just sit at Rick's desk and act like he was making notes on a legal pad like Rick was doing. Buddy has never forgotten Rick and doesn't comprehend that he's dead.*

As I've said before, Rick was always one for self promotion. But on one occasion, he used his influence to highlight the extraordinary work done by some of his most admired charities. One of our clients was a large billboard advertiser in the Southeastern United States. Rick did quite a bit of legal work for them before the Leon County Commission when a sign ordinance was being crafted. He traded out part of his fee for billboards around town that promoted four designated non-profits: Special Olympics, American Cancer Society, Alzheimer's Project, and Boys & Girls Clubs. He asked me to work up a marketing plan, engage a photographer, write copy, and set up photo shoots for each of the boards. The company gave us a total of eight locations around the county and would rotate the boards every couple of weeks to keep the messages fresh and provide each of the four charities with maximum exposure.

The first board we would set up would be easy, I thought. A favorite photo of mine that Rick kept in his office was of him and two children: A little boy with Down's Syndrome to his right and a little girl with no arms to his left, both around six years old. The shot was especially dear after hearing the story of the day it was taken. Rick had attended the Special Olympics games held for Leon County and several surrounding regions. He was a referee for some games and a walk along for some others. He had seen the little armless girl and had taken an immediate shine to her. He picked her up and placed her on his shoulders, wrapping his arms around her little thighs. Rick was six feet, four inches tall so I'm sure the view up there was fun and scary at the same time! He spent most of the day with her. He had her laughing so much that she got a bad case of the hiccups and he had to get a paper bag to help her breathe normally.

At the end of the event he posed with her and the little boy. After the picture was taken he offered up a hug to her, but she withdrew and looked down. "What's the matter, baby? Can't Mr. Rick give you a big hug for being the prettiest girl here?" he asked the child. She started to cry and mumbled through tears that she couldn't hug him back. His response to her came without pause or pity. "Well, sugar! I hug lots of women who don't hug me back, so don't let that bother you!" He grabbed her and gave her a very long bear hug. A week or so after the games, he received a handwritten letter from the little girl's mother who reported that before that day her daughter had barely spoken to anyone. Now she was a little chirping bird telling everyone about the big man who helped her "fly." The letter ended with the sentiment that she didn't know who Rick was, but to her and her daughter, he was an angel.

I contacted the Special Olympics coordinator at the state level to see if they could find out the name of the child. We needed her parents to sign a photo release and the handwritten letter had gone missing. It took almost a week of back and forth e-mails and phone calls before I got the sad answer. The mother and father had declined my request because their child was in kidney failure and not expected to live much longer. It would be too painful, they communicated through the charity's spokesman, to see her face smiling down all around town.

That billboard promotion would sit on the back burner for a while. I moved on to the American Cancer Society, Alzheimer's Project, and Boys & Girls Clubs promotions. I was fortunate to find a group of beautiful breast cancer survivors ranging from 23 to 60 years in age, including one of Rick's dear friends and former law partners, Glenda Thornton. I had pink polo shirts embroidered with the

Bateman Harden logo for each woman to wear in the picture. For the Alzheimer's Project board, Rick and his daughter, Callie, who had served on the non-profit's youth board, posed with an Alzheimer's patient and his wife. Rick posed alone with some young people from Boys & Girls Clubs, which proved to be the most tedious production. Go figure! Teenagers not showing up on time and acting out during the shoot!

Eventually, I got a young man and young lady lined up for the Special Olympics photo shoot with Rick on a local golf course that was hosting a tournament to benefit the organization. Not quite the same message conveyed as the one I had wanted to use, but the youngsters were engaging nonetheless.

We received phone calls daily from friends and clients saying that they were stalled in traffic and looked up to see Rick smiling down on them! It was such a great promotion and did a lot of good things for the individual organizations as well as for Bateman Harden. All of the boards listed sponsorship credit to the law firm along with our phone number and website address. Several new clients told me months after that they had seen one of the displays and it made a difference in their decision to come to our law firm. Like he'd demonstrated countless times, Rick Bateman knew how to promote himself better than anyone else could!

Rick was also very giving of his time and talent to the gay community. "It just pisses me off that because someone has a different sex life that they should be treated like outcasts!" he'd declare after hearing some shocking news report about the maiming or killing of a gay man. He had a soft spot in his heart for most social outcasts and would be the first to line up to represent them if the opportunity arose. I think he thought of himself as an outsider because of his strident persona.

"Jude! How many gay bars are in Tallahassee?" Rick shouted across the hall to me. "Excuse me?!" "Look it up, please. Julie's cousin is interested in opening one and I need to know what his competition will be." "When do you need the information?" Before Rick could answer me, Julie came in with her brother, Buddy, and another slender man who turned out to be her cousin, Tracy. We all stood around in the hallway chatting with one another (Buddy had retreated into Rick's office where he sat at his desk swinging his crossed leg like Rick did when he was on the phone), and then I realized Rick needed the information on bars now. I went back to my office and called an old friend who worked at the Division of Alcohol Beverages & Tobacco at the Department of Business Regulation. I asked him if he could find out which bars licensed in Tallahassee were known gay bars, since I doubted there was a selection box called "gay bar" in the permit questionnaire. It turned out that at the time there was only one known gay bar in Tallahassee. I gave the information to Rick. He grabbed his car keys and said to his little band of misfits, "Let's go!"

They drove all over town looking at several possible sites. Along the way Rick would pop in on friends, one of whom was in commercial real estate, introduced the three people in his car, ask for a beverage, and be on his way again.

*Rick and Tracy were in the front of his BMW and Buddy and I were in the back. He was singing some Frank Sinatra song and telling Tracy about how one of his best friends had been caught in a compromising position in a man's bathroom once, but since then he only liked women. He wasn't even thinking that what he was saying might be offensive to someone. We were all equal in his eyes, so he just told the story that seemed to fit the time and location of the moment. I laughed later thinking about how some of his friends and acquaintances might think it a bit strange that he was hanging out with a gay guy and a retarded man in his car that day!*

The promise of part-time jobs to the offspring of friends and relatives was another form of Rick's generosity and charity, if you will. He would hand out offers of jobs to them on the spur of the moment without consulting with me or giving me any advance warning of their arrival. "Hi, Ms. Burk. Where do I start?" the eager young man in front of my desk was inquiring. "Who are you?" "I'm Adam. Mr. Bateman said I could be your new runner." I asked him what his qualifications for the job were and when exactly he had been given the job. "Oh, I'm Ramona's son and he told my mom that I could be his runner when she told him I was looking for a part-time job this summer." The problem (in addition to the fact that I did all the hiring and firing for the firm), was that we already had a runner who was doing his job satisfactorily. As if on cue, Josh appeared at my door. He had overheard Adam telling me that he was our new runner and was wondering if he was being let go. "Do I need to look for a job somewhere else?" he asked me. "No! Go back out front and finish the assignment I gave you. This is not your concern!" I scolded him. Adam meanwhile, had taken a seat next to my desk and was playing with a Scottie dog statue near my computer. I grabbed it from his hand and told him to go to the conference room and have a seat until Mr. Bateman arrived.

Rick came strolling in about ten minutes later and saw Adam sitting in the conference room. "Hey, buddy! How's it going?" he called out to him. Adam took the greeting as a signal for him to go into Rick's office and sit down for a chummy chat with his "buddy." I was enjoying this whole scene immensely. I figured Rick deserved to be annoyed, just like I had been, and let the whole episode play out in his face. "Jude! Don't you have something for Adam to do?!" he yelled across the hall to me. I ignored him and picked up my phone to call the courthouse to check on a docket update on one of our cases. "Jude! Jude!" came the louder and louder pleas. I hung up when my call was complete and began to type out the information I'd just gathered. Rick could no longer stand it and walked across to my office and closed the door.

"Didn't you hear me?!" he screamed at me. "Mr. Bateman, lower your voice and speak to me in a civil tone," I cautioned him. "What are you going to do about Adam?" he asked. "Adam who?" "Are you crazy?! Adam in the next room!" I was having such a good time I hated to discontinue the interchange, but figured it was probably time to end the torment. "Mr. Bateman, I thought we had an agreement that I was the one in charge of hiring and firing employees around here. But today, not unlike many similar days in the past, a young man appeared before me and told me that he was our new runner, hired by you! You can imagine my confusion and that of Josh, our current runner! Maybe you should just go in your office and tell Adam that you were kidding, there is no job." Rick looked at me, confused about what he should say, and finally offered, "He's Ramona's son." *Not like you to lob me a soft one buckaroo,* I thought. "Oh, your former and perhaps, current girlfriend?" I sneered. Now he got it. "Well, just tell him to leave so I can get back to work!" he ordered. He opened the door and yelled to Adam that, "Ms. Burk has something to tell you," before I could fire one more shot directly between his eyes. And thus, I had to break it to Adam that there really wasn't a job, but he would be the first one I thought of if something came up in the way of an opening.

There were a few times when I let some of his "foundlings" stay for a specific assignment that I figured would put an end to their fantasy of a dream job working for their mother's boyfriend or their father's golf partner. One poor child was put in charge of mopping up the basement at Chesley House after a long, torrential rain had proven too much for the gutter system and flooded the entire area. We had quite a few old case files stored in boxes and stacked on the floor down there. So, after mopping the place up, the assignment was to re-box and re-label each of the six hundred or so that had been dampened by the flood water. He lasted until noon, when he took a lunch break and never came back. Another time, I dispatched the daughter of his then girlfriend to Rick's Alligator Point condo to clean out the refrigerator and collect his dirty laundry to take to the drycleaner in Tallahassee. She called me after she arrived at the condo and complained that the refrigerator smell was making her sick. I listened to her woes, commiserated with her situation, and told her to get back to work. We never saw her again.

As pathetic as the situations were with Rick handing out jobs like candy to these young people, the worst scenarios were when he hired his girlfriends to work at the law firm! One day he brought one in and announced to me that she would be helping him with the transition of some cases to Morgan & Morgan. Adding insult to injury, he let her occupy the office that had been my promised dream office with the crystal chandelier and storage closets! Oh, this one would be really interesting to watch play out! Hannah was pleasant enough and obviously a beautiful young lady, but I had no time or inclination to change the trajectory of where this would all lead. She came in when she wanted, took long lunch hours to go shopping at Rick's expense, worked for an hour in the afternoon or until she could convince Rick that it was time to go play, and never bid me a "Good morning!" "Good Afternoon!" or "See ya!" When the predicted demise of this little scheme came weeks later, it was Rick who complained that Hannah wasn't competent enough to do the job. "That's a shame," I said drolly.

# Chapter 15

## *The Eighth Commissioner*

If his first love was practicing law, a close second for Rick's professional ardor was representing an individual's or business's concern before governmental bodies. It came naturally to him. He had the gift of gab and the aptitude for turning an argument to his side of an issue. When he turned it on he was off the chart. He worked tirelessly with staff assigned to a particular matter, as well as their bosses. That said, he also wasn't afraid to leave body bags in his wake. Many times he would be brutal with a senior staff person who didn't agree with his point and then go over his or her head to get his way. The real testament to his savvy in the lobbying world was his ability to win back the affection and respect of the very people he stepped over. He could berate someone one day and the next day be sitting in that person's office sharing jokes and making plans for a lunch together. "He'd goad you into liking him again, even after putting an ice pick in the back of your head," one official confessed. "It didn't take long to figure out this was a guy who was bigger than the space he was filling."

The seven elected representatives on the Leon County Commission were so used to seeing him in the hallways and meeting chambers, they jokingly referred to him as "the eighth commissioner." The tag was one he enjoyed immensely and was useful to him in getting clients who needed a proponent for their issues. I remember chatting with another lobbyist at a social event. He was fascinated with Rick's unbridled access to elected officials and wondered how he did it. I told him that it was a combination of talent, brashness, and total honesty. Rick was who he was, but never lied to anyone. Everyone knew his word was his bond, even if he had to back off on a matter and let someone else declare victory.

> *He never put me in jeopardy and I found that to be exceptional. People who didn't know him thought he wasn't that guy. For years I was told to watch him, that he would do anything to win the day. But, he was a man of his word. I've had a lot of choir boys come through my office who haven't acted like that and would be the first to cast judgment on Rick. But Rick was solid, especially when issues heated up. If I asked him to take a pass on an issue, even some he could make real money on, he would. He said he wasn't here to create problems and damage.*

Because I had lobbied the Florida Legislature when I was an association executive, Rick would use me as his Devil's Advocate when rehearsing a presentation. We'd yell at each other, contend that our respective point was more convincing than the other's, and end the debate with a "high five." I'd type up a bullet point list in eighteen point type so he could easily refer to it if needed. He would then drive me crazy with having me constantly calling the commissioners' staff trying to poll the votes. He'd want that particular piece of information before heading out the door so he could share it with the commissioners who were still wavering on their position before their meeting began. That was another thing that set Rick apart from other lobbyists. He would reveal his game plan to each commissioner separately, telling of his arguing points and advising how many votes he had lined up. By doing this, he was giving everyone an opportunity to work through their concerns and know what to expect when the official meeting started. No one ever got blindsided by Rick Bateman.

> *I came to know Rick when I was a young man coming up the ranks on county policy analysis and writing commission agenda items on the Board's most pressing issues. Rick was a fixture in the chambers. You don't miss Rick. Who is this guy? Half Earnest Hemingway and half Jack Nicholson? It was over a period of about seventeen years that we became friends. I knew he was fascinating and clearly smart, but in my business you keep a cautious perspective on issues, especially where lobbyists are concerned, so I withheld my opinion on Rick. As I moved up the county administration I became much more involved in issues, and the more I worked with him the more clearly I got to know who he was, and then it was done. We became very good friends.*

*Everybody in the political world has political friends and then they have real friends. I learned from Rick that I just have friends. He didn't put them in a category. If there was someone who was important to him politically, but wasn't friendly to him, he wasn't going to pretend to be their friend and later make campaign contributions to them. But if you were his client, he would kill for you. Many times I sat back watching him and thought, "If I ever get in trouble, he's my guy!"*

The gratification of putting people and a deal together on particularly contentious issues was irresistible to Rick, even when he had no dog in the fight! One presented itself to him by merely being in the right place at the right time:

*There was an issue that was probably in the top five of white hot ones I've dealt with. A large, multi-national company had indicated its interest in coming to town and the board was considering financial incentives for the company to relocate to Leon County, not an uncommon practice. But sometimes there comes a time where you have to draw a line to determine if it makes sense. A politician can simply write a check, and without any real effort create high paying jobs for the community. So it has an almost irresistible political appeal. The downside from a policy standpoint is that it tends not to work a lot. Companies that come with incentives can leave and get more incentives elsewhere. It's a dangerous game.*

*As we were at the negotiation table, the price kept getting higher in what they wanted in incentives. There were millions in cash in addition to buildings and other things. The CEO of the company and others who wanted the deal to happen, including bankers, Realtors, and a contingent of eight or nine suits from other major businesses and economic development were pressing for it. The company was headquartered in Holland and their expertise was not proven at the time and the technology they were presenting was new. So we took a position at the staff level that enough is enough and presented our position to the board that we didn't think that writing millions of dollars for the company's relocation was a good deal.*

*The board was workshopping the issue prior to their formal meeting. We'd made our staff recommendations and hoped they would agree, but were willing to let whatever happened, happen. At a brief recess before the commission was to convene for a vote, I noticed that all the people who had been there to argue for the company were no longer in the commission chambers. I went down past the commission offices and looked inside Commissioner Dan Winchester's office. Rick was sitting behind*

*Dan's desk with his feet up and the room was full of those people. They were clearly lobbying Dan, but Rick was holding court. By now, there was at least a year's worth of work done and Rick clearly had no involvement up to this point. But, he was using the opportunity to organize the group and get Dan's vote for the economic development folks since he was on their board at that time, I believe. He looked up and saw me and looked quizzically at me. I went back into the chamber and told the County Administrator that Rick was in the room with all the players. He told me to go back and tell Rick that this was not one he should get involved with. At that point, Rick had gotten Dan's vote and it was going to be a 4-3 decision. I went back and motioned to him to come out in the hall. I told him not to get involved in this one. He said, "Oh, alright. You want me to undo it?" I said, "Yeah."*

*By now, the commissioners were up on the dais ready to start their formal proceedings. Rick walked up behind the County Administrator and told him he didn't know he wasn't supposed to get involved. He motioned to Dan, who stepped down and came over to Rick. Rick whispered in his ear and then Dan went back up to his seat, and pounding the table declared, "We should not do this!" He got really emotional. So at this point the county wasn't in the deal for the cash incentives. It was a really big issue in the community afterward.*

*After the meeting, Dan got in an elevator, and some of the suits were in there, and people outside could hear them arguing. I asked Rick what he had said to Dan. "I told him they didn't need him, he wasn't important so they didn't need his vote anymore."*

Not long after that night, Winchester was arrested for stalking, aggravated assault, kidnapping, and domestic battery against his estranged wife and was committed to Florida State Hospital for mental health treatment. I'm not saying that Rick drove the man to violence and mental illness, but he certainly added fuel to an already simmering fire.

Manipulating fragile egos wasn't Rick's only dubious craft. From a story shared by a close friend and business associate, he also seemed to have the ability to make warm beer change to cold on demand:

*I represented Waffle House in their closings at different locations. They were looking into opening one of their restaurants in the small town of Midway in Gadsden County, near the I-10 interchange. The company's executive was a good friend and asked me to recommend a lawyer/lobbyist and I said Rick. He was the only one I knew who could be that charming country boy wearing flannel shirts and saying some "Aw shucks," and later don his Armani suits and be a polished sophisticate. He took the assignment and worked the issue behind the scenes for us.*

*We all went to the final hearing before the local commission. My friend came down from Atlanta, dressed to the nines. When she walked into the small meeting room, she said to me that she felt she had stepped back in time. One female commissioner had a hat on with a sales tag hanging from it! Rick was up front talking to the commissioners and charming them. We won their unanimous vote.*

*We decided to celebrate. A mutual friend in Bainbridge, Georgia wanted us to come there because someone he knew was running for office and he wanted us to meet him. I was the designated driver. On the way, my friend wanted to stop for beer. Rick went into a convenience store and bought a six pack. She only drank one beer every ten minutes or so and the other beers would get warm. So, we'd stop at another convenience store along the way and Rick would go in and talk the attendant into exchanging one new cold one from a six pack for one of the warm ones and they'd do it! My friend had cold beers all the way up and back!*

*I drove them all night and don't even remember all the places we went. I ended up having to drive them both home. I got Rick to his house where he fell out on the lawn. He stumbled into his garage where Old Joe, his hunting dog was sleeping. Rick ended up sleeping on the dog bed with him. My friend stayed in her hotel room most of the next day trying to recover in order to get to New Orleans the following day for a business appointment.*

The Leon County Commission and the Tallahassee City Commission meetings were televised on local stations. Rick would watch them to determine when he should head out the door and attend the meetings so he wouldn't waste time sitting and waiting for his item to be addressed. When he would leave, I'd keep an eye on our television monitor to catch him in action when he would approach the speaker's podium. Several times I caught him standing behind someone, impatiently waiting his turn at the microphone, and adjusting his male parts as a nervous habit to keep himself under control. *Oh, God. There he goes again!* I would groan to myself. It wasn't until I shared this mortifying idiosyncrasy with his stepmother that I found out it was a Bateman trait! Rick came by it honestly, having emulated the other men in the family! Couldn't they have chosen something else, like eye rolling or head scratching?!

"Do you know anything about internet cafes?" Rick asked me one day. "I do not," I confessed. "Well, we're going to be representing one," he said as he walked into his office and took a phone call. I went on line and researched what an internet café was. There was no standard description of one, but there were dozens of newspaper articles about police investigations of internet café operations throughout the state. I printed some and waited for Rick to finish his phone call to take them to him. He glanced at a couple and said, "Yeah. That's what we need to figure out. We want to make sure that the one we represent complies with local codes since there isn't a state law outlawing them."

We continued our conversation over the next hour. I questioned why he would want to get involved in something that could be shady and quite possibly cost him his license to practice law. "Because there's an obscene amount of legal fees to be made, that's why!" he exclaimed. I knew only too well that he and the law firm were in desperate need of some income, but I didn't feel comfortable about this new client. "Jude, you worry too much. I'm not going to do anything unlawful and you won't be involved in any way," he assured me.

Rick contracted the services of his old friend from law enforcement, whom he had used during the Joe Francis case, to act as his go between with police:

> *It was such a gray area about whether they were legal or not. Rick used me for my respected reputation in law enforcement to be a go between with Sheriff Campbell. The idea was to legitimize his client's place as not being shady. He said that he wanted everything they did to be transparent. Rick's attitude was, "If they want my guys to leave, they will. We just need some warning if they do." There had recently been a raid on a bingo parlor and Rick wanted to avoid anything like that. There was a lot of breast*

*beating going on in communities throughout the state and some politicians used the issue as their own personal soap box. In some places there was a shake down, where some of the people making the most noise about how bad the cafes were had offered to be quiet for a cut of the action.*

*I offered some security advice. The client had wanted a uniformed deputy at the location at all times, but the Sheriff didn't feel comfortable about it since it still hadn't been made clear about what the places were. The prevailing attitude was that the law enforcement guys didn't have a personal stake in messing with the internet cafes, but if laws were passed to make them illegal, they would arrest people.*

As much as he tried to ensure that our client was conforming to whatever requirements local government instituted to keep their cafe open, too many other café operators were giving the business a bad name. By the summer of 2012, it became apparent that the days of internet cafes were numbered. Georgia had just passed a law prohibiting their operation and word on the street was that Florida wasn't far behind. Leon County had already passed a local ordinance requiring annual permitting. The ordinance gave a grace period upon adoption for those cafes already operating to comply with registration requirements and to apply for a permit. Only ten cafes would be permitted in the county, so those already up and running got the first shot at getting one. Our client was one of them and they received a permit without issue.

A location requirement in the adopted ordinance was specific. No café could be within 500 feet of schools, churches, senior centers, or community centers. Nor could one café be closer than 5,000 feet from another café, unless they were already operating in a closer proximity on the date the ordinance was adopted. If they were and they successfully completed a registration for a permit, they would be allowed to operate in the closer range. A few weeks after our client's café was permitted, Allied Veterans of the World opened a store next door. Rick cried foul and approached commissioners with his objection to the store being allowed to get a permit and operate next to his client's.

*Rick was wounded and angry about Allied because the ordinance said no one could be next door and he was livid that the county allowed them to open. The window for legal operation of internet cafes was closing and I think everyone in the business recognized it was a short shelf life. Folks were making a lot of money. The county's standpoint was that the window was closing, but until it did, operators could go crazy making themselves rich. But they needed to understand that the window WAS closing.*

*Many people thought because we were friends that I would roll over regularly. But to his credit, we agreed to disagree on the internet café thing. I took Allied to task before one of the commission meetings and asked them how much money was generated in their cafes and how much was going to veterans. They couldn't tell me. I told them that I didn't want them to come to my county and make it look like they were doing all these pro-veteran things and painting me as being against veterans.*

Rick filed a lawsuit for our client against Allied. A hearing on the case was scheduled for the week after he returned from the South Eastern Conference (SEC) championship football game in Atlanta, and he was going to win. He had been masterful in his deposition of Allied's representatives and had enough ammunition to blow them out of the water. But, he died and the hearing was cancelled and the case dropped. Just three months after his death, however, Allied Veterans of the World's internet cafes throughout the state were raided by law enforcement. Representatives of the fake charity were accused of scheming to defraud the public and governmental agencies by misrepresenting how much of its proceeds were donated to charities affiliated with the Veterans Administration.

The Florida Legislature outlawed all internet cafes during that same time. Lieutenant Governor Jennifer Carroll resigned her office after the Department of Law Enforcement discovered that she was connected to Allied Veterans of the World through public relations work her firm had done for them, including her personal appearance in a television commercial supporting the group's good works for veterans. I just know that if Rick had still been around he would have worked with investigators on their case and provided the evidence he had already gathered on the group. It galled him that his good friend, Julie, had been working for years to set up Veterans Villages to provide veterans with vocational job training, affordable housing and family health care without claiming a dime for herself; while the Allied sham put millions of dollars into the pockets of con artists by fronting the name of veterans.

It was all about fair play to Rick. If others played fair with him, he would grant them the same. But if they didn't, he would utilize all his resources to make them regret it.

# Chapter 16

## *Nothing Left to Lose*

The day I had been dreading had arrived. A hearing was being held in Family Court on Rick's proposed modification to his Marital Settlement Agreement (MSA) with Donna, his first wife, and I was to be a witness for Rick. The monthly installments on their settlement that he was required to pay, in addition to mortgage payments on the home he had surrendered to her after their divorce, were delinquent. He had petitioned the court to modify the agreement so the costs wouldn't be such a drain on him. As hard as I'd tried to remain separate from his personal life, especially his dealings with Donna and the girls, I was now being pulled in to it.

It wasn't that Rick didn't make money. He did...lots of it. But most of the funds were used up in loan payments for the various corporations he had created when acquiring property or setting up land trusts for his daughters. Since the real estate market was at an all time low, he was unable to liquidate any of his holdings to come up with enough cash to honor his commitments. The fact that we hadn't been paid in full by several high profile clients (who Rick had refused to haunt for payments), left the Bateman Harden law firm in a tenuous situation when it came to payroll. More than once, the bank balance was insufficient to cover salaries and operating expenses. On paper we were in high cotton, but the reality was that we were cash poor.

Rick used the law firm's American Express card as his personal expense account to which he would charge everything from groceries to gift purchases for his lovers. At the end of the month it was all the same as far as cash flow was concerned. There were more bills than there was bank balance to pay them. It was such a foreign experience to me. David and I worked hard for many years to be debt free, and now I was in a situation that caused me to lose sleep worrying about making payments to debtors that weren't my responsibility! Adding to the worry was the fact that I had written personal checks from my own bank account to cover payroll and insurance for staff so the business wouldn't be interrupted and clients wouldn't be denied their legal representation.

"Will you drive so I can get my thoughts together?" Rick asked me as the time to head out for the courthouse arrived. "Sure." His request was not a small thing and I knew it. Rick always drove, mostly in his big BMW that I hated. It had all the bells and whistles of modern distraction one could imagine. The driver's area looked like a plane cockpit to me with all the red flashing lights and wrap around dashboard with dials and audible messages. My 1995 Mercedes was my dream car. I bought her new, just off the boat from Germany, and she ran like a top at seventeen years old. I named her "Mercy" for the state of grace I was in when driving her...always safe. She and I had the same malady; a good strong engine, but some body deterioration. The thought of buying a newer car never entered my mind. Rick, on the other hand, had to have the newest, most technologically enhanced machine available to man. His request for me to drive meant that he was seriously distracted and didn't want to get behind the wheel of a powerhouse machine.

When we stopped at a traffic light a few blocks before the courthouse, the fuel pump let out a low moan that sounded like a cow's moo. "Sorry about that," I said. "She does that when she's cold. It will pass when I drive a few more blocks." "I like it," Rick said as he stared out the side window. "It comforts me." I thought he was kidding and laughed a bit. When his body remained rigid in his sideway posture, I realized he was serious. Who would have thought Rick Bateman would have a Zen moment?

The hearing was not all that long, but it was tense to say the least. The judge was courteous to Rick, but I could tell she wasn't impressed with his plea of poverty. When it came time for me to testify I verified that Bateman Harden was broke and that I didn't know how we would make the upcoming payroll. The judge seemed a bit shocked by what I said and asked me to verify it. I did. A few more questions and then I was dismissed. I glanced over at Donna as I walked back to my seat and felt sick to my stomach. I hated being in the middle of this drama and was conflicted by my feelings of loyalty to Rick against my sympathy for her in having to revisit the divorce.

When the hearing was over, Rick said he would walk back to the office. I was physically shaken by my own experience in the courtroom and understood that he was probably feeling many times worse than I. The judge advised that she would have a ruling in the next few days and I'm pretty sure Rick knew that it wouldn't be favorable to him.

He walked into my office about thirty minutes past the time it should have taken him to make the trip from the courthouse on foot. "Are you okay?" I asked. "I just spoke with Bill Brownstone," he responded. That name meant one thing. Rick was thinking of filing for bankruptcy. "And?" I asked. "We need to pull some things together for me to take over to him on Tuesday," was his response. "Rick! Tell me what you're thinking! Don't give me some instruction on what we need to do!" "I'm sorry. I think I need to go for a run. I'll see you tomorrow." With that, he was out the door and driving away in the "Batmobile."

It was no easy task to assemble the financial records of a man who created and disassembled corporations like a toddler erecting and then knocking down building blocks. Dozens of bookkeepers, secretaries, and business managers had preceded me and each had his or her own way of keeping records. Translating all of those records and reconciling them to bank statements and stock entries challenged my sanity. Rick was insatiable when it came to buying the latest technology for his personal use, but he was miserly in approving the purchase of new hardware and software to manage his businesses. The old Quickbooks reports were reliant on the skill and work ethic of whichever staff person had compiled them. Since Rick was a demanding but detached task master, I found most of the records to be incomplete and useless.

Five days and sleepless nights later, the three volumes of 5-inch thick notebooks were assembled for Rick's meeting with his bankruptcy attorney. Before we left for the meeting, I asked Rick if he wanted to go through the information with me so he could be prepared for any questions that might come up. "Why? You'll be there and you can tell him what he wants, can't you?" was his response. "I'm not the one filing for bankruptcy! Don't you want to know the real story on your situation?" He just looked at me with an expression that said, "Do you really think I don't know that I'm in deep shit?" We walked outside and Rick went directly to my car and got in the passenger side. Once again, I was the driver to the appointment to reality.

Anyone who thinks bankruptcy is the answer to their financial problems is delusional. It does not render one debt free and clean. It does not give peace to a troubled soul. It does not allow one to pass "Go" without any penalty. It does open up a Pandora's Box of bill collectors, mortgage processors, and creditors who can pull the plug on daily operations, rendering a smooth running business into a Dickensian work environment.

*Worst thing I ever had to do was to file for foreclosure on the farm. He would put shit off to the last minute and I don't think he was capable of winning anymore. He was the bread winner for his family – the publishing of intent to foreclosure I filed, his Daddy had to read it. He couldn't maintain that level and that made him doubt himself.*

~~~~~

*He was very sad. There were months when he didn't want to talk and would be quiet for a whole hour. When he and Donna were going*

184

*through their settlement agreement he acted full of regret and had a lot on his shoulders.*

~~~~~

*Rick's identity and sense of self worth was dependent on being a financial success. It wasn't the money, but the image and his ego. When things went downhill financially, he couldn't bear it.*

In the midst of all the turmoil surrounding the filing for bankruptcy, two other major events were playing themselves out. Rick had been trying to proffer a deal with the note holders of the Chesley House. There was a balloon payment coming due that was impossible for Rick to pay, so several meetings were held to work out some creative alternatives for us to stay in our offices while the ownership reverted back to the note holders. After months of haggling with no agreement being reached, eviction proceedings had begun. I was again faced with moving the law firm to a different location. I called my good friend, Chip, who specialized in commercial real estate, and asked him to look for some viable lease options for me to view. Over a six week period we looked at dozens of office buildings. Each had its own set of issues that eliminated them from consideration.

Part of the original plan for our move to the Chesley House was to establish a Morgan & Morgan branch office in Tallahassee. Rick and John Morgan were old friends and had discussed the possibility of joining forces. Rick had met John through his college sweetheart, Laura's, family. Her brother was one of John's best friends and roommate at the University of Florida. The arrangement would be for Morgan's personal injury law practice to occupy part of the Chesley building. Rick would head up a new Business Trial Group civil law practice under the Morgan flag in the other part. Bateman Harden would be retained by Rick to handle some small cases and to provide legal counsel to Southern Communities Foundation. I would manage Bateman Harden and Chesley Management, LLC, the corporation to which Rick assigned his ownership interest in Chesley House. With the rents collected from the new businesses, it would be easy to cover the note payments and monthly expenses for the LLC.

In order to test the waters on Morgan's branching out to civil litigation, it was decided that Rick would divide his time between Tallahassee and Orlando. He would join other high octane legal talent to form the Business Trial Group at the Morgan mother ship in downtown Orlando and set up residency in nearby Winter Park. Rick took with him several of the larger Bateman Harden cases as his "dowry" to kick start the operation. He was given his own staff of assistants for his legal work. I was in Tallahassee holding down Bateman Harden and overseeing the other facets of Rick's life, while managing Chesley Management and coordinating the corporate records of Southern Communities Foundation. In the meantime, efforts were underway for Morgan's personal injury branch to open in Tallahassee.

Rick's presence in Orlando was felt immediately. Team members were assigned to a list of cases and he made it clear what he expected from each of them. The young attorneys working under him were awestruck by his depth of knowledge and his rabid guardianship of "his guys." Once you were on his team he'd step in front of a train for you. "Even being a senior guy, if you needed help, he'd show up," relayed one of Rick's favorite young lawyers at Morgan. "If opposing counsel tried to use their age and experience to intimidate one of us, he would get in their face about it. In my experience, there are very few people like that. He added a ton of color to your life, mostly for the better. Life was more interesting when he was here."

As they saw the wit and wisdom of Rick, so too did the young lawyers see his intolerance for mistakes and his assignment of blame to the nearest target:

> *We were given this paralegal whose competence on a scale of one to ten was a two! He was from New York City and had survived the World Trade Center attacks, so he probably got jobs out of pity. We were preparing for one of the largest cases we'd taken so far. Rick and I split the list of witnesses and the paralegal was to prepare the Q & A in tabbed notebooks for each of us. He really fucked it up.*

> *Rick got his notebook first and started screaming at me. I told him I had instructed the paralegal on what to do, but he had messed it all up. Rick shot back that it was my fault for giving the assignment to him. I shouted back that I had to give it to him since he was the paralegal assigned to the case, and I was also pissed about the mess because I was trying to get ready for trial too. He told me I should have*

187

*known better than to give it to that guy so he*
*was blaming me. I was dying laughing because*
*he had to vent and was going off on me!*

Sadly, the plan for Morgan and Rick to join forces in
Tallahassee went up in flames after Rick chose the wrong
time, place, and victim for his drunken antics. He regularly
hosted after work get togethers at a favorite bar near his
apartment. Young staff members, seasoned attorneys, old
friends, and anyone else who looked interesting to him were
welcomed to Rick Bateman's party. As the booze flowed, he
dazzled everyone with his tales of war in courtrooms, as well
as sagas of his hunting expertise in the field and in the
bedroom. These gatherings emboldened him to be loose and
unguarded with his foul mouth and invasion of others'
personal space.

The annual Morgan & Morgan dinner was being held at a
very nice hotel and attendance was considered mandatory.
Before dinner, drinks and conversation were shared and
Rick was getting cozy with several female employees,
including grabbing the backside of one of the personal injury
lawyers. She took exception to his behavior and reported it
to the bosses. I found out about the upsetting situation when
I read through Rick's incoming e-mails the next day. The
computer systems had been set up so both Rick and I had
Morgan e-mail addresses in addition to our Bateman Harden
ones. I saw whatever appeared on his screen in Orlando. The
communication from the Morgan offices made it clear that
his "inappropriate behavior with one of the female attorneys
last night sealed the deal" on their decision to not share
office space. They would still be opening a branch in

Tallahassee, but would find their own location away from Bateman Harden. "I had him written up for the file, but I didn't fire him," John Morgan revealed. "But, he knew he was under observation."

I stared at the computer screen in disbelief. How could he be so cavalier and jeopardize this great opportunity handed to him? What could have motivated him? Then I thought that perhaps it was all a big misunderstanding. Yes, Rick was a "touchy feely" kind of guy and his hands had found their way onto my body occasionally, but never in a sexual or lascivious manner. Some people are put off by that kind of familiarity and maybe that's all this had been. I was sure it was unintentional. I clung to that thought to get me through the day.

Rick hadn't called or e-mailed me by 5:00 p.m., so I called him on his cell phone. He picked up on the first ring. "Hey! Sorry I haven't called today. Everything okay?" I was a little put off by his laid back speech. "Yes, everything's okay. How are you?" "Good, really good." "I saw the e-mail from the Morgan people about last night." Silence. "Rick?" More silence. Finally, he spoke in a tone that was alien to me. "I'm sorry she was upset. I'll apologize." That was it. Nothing more. He said goodbye and told me that he was going to stay in Orlando through the weekend to tend to some matters that needed his attention. "Call me if you need me," he offered. I hung up and felt the earth opening up beneath me. This was bad.

Now that the bankruptcy had been filed, all creditors had been notified and their responses began in earnest. Some were granted a Relief from Stay, meaning they could move forward with foreclosure actions, and others were merely lining up to be high on the list of those paid when any funds were recovered by the court. I had to find a company who would come by the law firm and Rick's homes to appraise the belongings so the court would know how much cash the sale of the items would bring. When I told Rick this, he freaked out. "You mean, I got to declare my furniture and everything?!" he cried. "Your furniture, your dishes, your artwork, your fishing gear, your rugs, your head phones...everything!" I declared. "Unfucking believable!" he responded, and threw himself down on his chair. "What did you think would happen when you filed? Did you not know that anything of value is fair game to give over to your creditors?" No response. He got up and left the building, not returning until late the next day.

In the morning, I met the appraisers at the office. I explained to them that only a few things on Rick's desk were personal items, everything else belonged to the law firm and was, therefore, not available to the court for liquidation. After a very brief stay, we drove over to Sixth Avenue to review the household goods and furnishings there. Rick's car was gone so I figured he wasn't in the house. When we got inside there was no sign of him and I gave the appraisers full reign to go through the house and tally up the belongings. Again, it was a quick walk through and we were done. I told them about the Millstone house and the Alligator Point condo and provided them with an inventory of items at each place. The list was less than half a page long, since Rick hadn't been at either property for months.

When Rick finally came back to the office, he asked me what the net value of his personal belongings was according to the appraisers. I told him around $28,000.00. "Are you fucking kidding me?!" he screamed. "Rick, it's a good thing. The appraisers evaluate everything at liquidation value for quick sales. You can buy your things back from the court and not have to worry about replacing anything," I explained. "Are you sure? If that's so, let's do it right away before anyone else can." With that, he was in his office and on his phone to his bankruptcy attorney who confirmed that the trustee was willing to take $25,000 for the personal property, which represented a little more than ten percent off the liquidation number. He also told Rick that he would have to sign a promissory note with the court and make full payment within 90 days. The note was signed and Rick was back on the road. He had a trial in Naples in another week and wanted to get all of his staff together in Orlando for a final run through of the case. "I've got some really good people going with me and I think we'll hit it out of the park!" he announced to me as he left. He blew me a kiss, told me that he loved me, and raced out of the parking lot. I sure hoped he would hit a home run. He needed $25,000.00 fast!

The clock was ticking loudly on the days I had left to find suitable office space to move into. It was now Thursday and we had to vacate the Chesley House by Monday. Rick was gone and I had to take action. I called Chip and told him I needed to see anything that was out there and needed to see it today! He told me he'd call me right back. When he called he told me that there were offices available just down the street from Chesley House on Gadsden Street. As soon as he described it I let out a scream! The Moore Bass Consulting executive building! The same building where I originally interviewed for the job as Rick Moore's Executive Assistant! And the same building where I had met with Rick and Karen to discuss plans to keep Clay's projects going forward when he could no longer come to work! After downsizing of staff and operations, Rick and Karen moved their executive operations to the big engineering building across the street and put their former offices up for lease. "Yes!" I shouted to Chip. "Can I see it now?" He told me he'd contact the real estate management company who had the listing to see if he could get a key. Within an hour we were walking through the building and I was time traveling to other, less complicated days. The rent was do-able, but I didn't know how I would come up with the deposit. I asked Chip to intervene on that issue and let me know if I could make plans for a move that weekend.

As soon as I got back to Chesley House I was hailed by our paralegal to come to her office. I went in and she said that "some man" had been in the building while I was gone and put notes on furniture and other fixtures. She said she didn't know who he was, but she didn't know what to do about it. I told her it was okay and I would look into it. I saw some of the notes on some furniture items in my office and immediately knew what was going on. When the note holders had moved their offices from the big house to the smaller one out back, they had left several pieces of furniture. They were listed in the original note, some being considered part of the purchase and some were "loaners" since they had no space for them in their smaller quarters. Now that we were being evicted and there was no purchase, they were tagging the items that were not to be moved out when our moving crew showed up. Seeing those tags made it all the more real that this situation had now moved into the desperate mode.

I called Rick at his Orlando office and told him about the Moore Bass office lease. At first, he was reluctant and said he didn't think it would work for us. "It's perfect for us!" I yelled at him. "We'll have more than enough space for us, our files, and an extra office or two for expansion." I told him about the monthly rent and security deposit I needed in forty-eight hours. "Okay. If you want it, Jude, that's all that matters. Do it." "Thanks. Do you have any money you can send me so I can consummate the deal?" He started talking to someone who had come into his office and hung up on me. I sighed deeply and shook my head. I wasn't insulted by the hang up...Rick did that all the time. He did it to me and just about everyone else. When he finished with his side of a conversation, or when he got interrupted, he simply hung up the phone and dispensed with any "goodbye" formalities.

It was Friday morning and the moving company had just left with the large items we were taking with us. The items would stay on their truck overnight. The movers would come back the next morning at the new location to unload it. The Bateman Harden law firm was now reduced to me, two interns who worked on days when they had no law school classes, a part-time bookkeeper, and a paralegal. Each of them had done yeoman's work in boxing up files, office supplies, artwork, and personal belongings. My husband had also participated by coming to the building after he'd put in a full day's work at his own job and disassembled and strapped down some of Rick's antiques. Chip and I spoke by phone for the last time and I thanked him for his help. "Good Lord willing, we'll be boxed up by the end of the day and ready for our move into the new offices tomorrow," I told him. At this point, I was now dealing directly with the management company on the payment of the deposit and getting our keys.

I should have known better than to think the lease signing and rent payment would go easily. That Friday was spent on countless phone calls and e-mails with the leasing company on lease verbiage, lease terms, furniture being left in the building, and the exact amount of rents needed for a deposit. Rick was on his way back from Orlando, but wouldn't be in town until after close of business. I called our computer guys and confirmed that they would be arriving at Chesley House the next morning at 8:00 a.m. to disconnect our computer system. If something didn't happen soon, we would be out on the street in hours! I picked up the phone and called Karen Bass, who once again became my personal hero and promised to intercede with the leasing company.

Promises of getting the revised lease to me were unfulfilled by 6:00 p.m. The last e-mail I sent to the leasing company was filled with my anger and frustration. Everyone who had been a part of the leasing negotiations for Gadsden was out of town until Monday. I was sulking on the floor of my office at Chesley House since my furniture had already been put on the truck for delivery to Gadsden Street the next morning. One more glance at my watch and that was it for me. I got up, turned off the lights, and walked to my car. I was physically and emotionally spent. My brain was numb as I tried to access any tidbit of information that would be useful in begging for an extension of time at Chesley.

As I turned onto Wakulla Springs Road for the final segment of my drive home, the darkness surrounding me put me in a state of surrender. I pulled over to the side of the road and called Rick on his cell phone. He sounded happy.

"Hey! What's…" Before he could finish his sentence, I started talking. "I've had it! I'm done!" I cried into the phone. "What?! Wait a minute, baby! What's wrong?" I ran through the litany of insults and aggravations that had comprised my miserable day and concluded with the same, "I've had it!" Rick was trying to calm me down and told me that he'd make some phone calls and take care of everything. "Just don't leave me," he begged. "Go home, have some wine with David and let me handle all this. I'm sorry I've let you down, but we'll be okay. Okay?!" I didn't know what to say. I was too tired to care. "Okay," was all I could get out.

The next morning I received a text from Rick around 7:00 a.m. He was meeting the owner of the leasing company at our new location to sign the lease, make the payment, and get the keys. I was to go to Chesley House and take care of the last minute arrangements to have the computers shut down and then meet him at Gadsden Street. "Finally, you're acting like the man who gives a shit," I said out loud to the phone screen. When I made it to our new offices before noon, Rick was standing in the parking lot. "Here are the keys. I'll see you Monday." I took the keys and shook my head as he jumped into his truck and sped away. He was dressed in camouflage, so I guessed that he was headed to Woodbine for the remainder of the weekend.

I didn't see Rick that Monday, or Tuesday. The staff and I were busy unpacking and arranging furniture in offices when my private phone line rang. I was upstairs with our paralegal setting up files when I saw my extension flash on her phone screen. I had forwarded the line so I wouldn't have to run up and down the stairs when and if Rick called me. My arthritic knees were screaming for rest and that's the last thing I could give them. I picked up the phone. "This is Jude Burk." It was someone from security at an apartment complex near Gainesville. Rick's BMW had been parked in a "no parking zone" for a couple of days. It was unlocked and a large amount of cash was inside. They also found one of Rick's pistols under the driver's seat. My name and contact information in case of emergency was in his glove box. I transferred the call back to my office downstairs where I could speak privately. I told the caller that I didn't know where Mr. Bateman was, but I would try him on his cell phone. They advised that they knew Rick was an attorney and they would hold onto the money and gun until they heard from me. The call concluded with my promise to let them know when I heard from Rick. I sent three text messages to Rick's cell phone over the next hour. The last one was simply, "Send me OK just so I know you're alive somewhere." Ten minutes later, the message, "OK", popped up on my cell screen.

I would like to say that I hadn't a clue about Rick's condition, but that wouldn't be the truth. I knew his prescription drug use had spun out of control and I had put enough pieces of the puzzle together to not come to any other conclusion than the one I was now confronting. This was a "lost weekend" and I was sure it wasn't the first he'd had recently. If anyone had asked me if I had ever seen Rick take anything that wasn't prescribed, I could honestly say "no." But, I had suffered through a relationship with a drug abuser and knew one when I saw one. I went upstairs and told the staff we all deserved the afternoon off and sent everyone home. After they'd gone, I went to the bathroom and threw up.

On Wednesday, Rick arrived at the office around 9:00 a.m., driving his BMW. Whatever had transpired at that apartment complex had obviously been resolved. We never spoke of it. We were enablers to one another that way. He enabled me to continue believing that all would be well in Batemanland, and I enabled him to live a life that scared the hell out of me. He came into my office and asked me to call everyone into the conference room for an update on cases. He looked fine. Once again, the Bateman steely constitution had kicked in and he was functioning in high gear. He was working with our interns on a case that had multiple moving parts and was throwing directions and case references out at machine gun speed. I loved this Rick Bateman. The one who had a game plan, predicted which direction would have the most efficient termination, and knew when to strike and when to lay low. He could drive his staff crazy with his demands and unkind remarks when anyone appeared to be unprepared for an impromptu rundown of the merits of a case. He was magic and could make something out of nothing just by zeroing in on the prize.

Everyone worked late and no one complained. Now that we had to share Rick with the Morgan firm, we were like little puppies waiting for our master to return home and give us the attention we craved. When it was time for him to once again hit the road and drive back to Orlando, he shouted, "I love y'all!" to the staff upstairs and motioned for me to come with him as he walked to his car. "I'm going to kick some ass in Naples next week and have a big payday. I'll be back up here for Thanksgiving so make sure the stone crab claws are ordered. Think about what you want for Christmas. This has been a helluva year and I want to give you something special." "Mr. Bateman, the only thing I want for Christmas is for you to start taking care of yourself and decide what you want to be when you grow up. You can't keep up this pace and it's time for you to either move permanently to Orlando or come back here full time." He looked at me for a minute and then broke the tender moment we were having with that caustic cackle, "Jesus, Jude! I was thinking of a spa weekend or gold bracelet or something!"

I had always regretted our penurious situation at Chesley House. I had longed to decorate the place for the holidays with miles of garland on the white picket fence, golden ivy draped along the front stairway, and a Christmas tree in the front window decked out in gold and silver ornaments with gingerbread men dangling from every branch. The place begged for it! I had champagne taste with a beer budget, so I scrimped on our office supply purchases to free up some "play money" for a few potted poinsettias with gold tipped leaves spread throughout the offices. Now that we were living a little more within our means at Gadsden Street, I was feeling upbeat and optimistic about the New Year, especially since Rick had three cases in the next three months that promised a fee split over $1 million! I decided that this year I would dig into my own pocket and decorate our new offices in a style that would say, "Welcome home!" as my Christmas gift to Rick. I knew he'd be attending the SEC Championship football game in Atlanta in a few weeks and that would be the weekend I would choose to decorate the place to surprise him when he returned the following Monday.

The case in Naples was a complicated one, but Rick had already predicted an early settlement. It would be a jury trial, which was his bread and butter, and he felt the staff he had been given would help set the stage for his stellar performance. He called me throughout the week on Bateman Harden matters and ended each call with, "I can't wait to go to Naples and show John Morgan what I'm worth!" I was confused by the reference. Of course John knew what he was worth. He and the Morgan team were working together on some pretty big cases and Rick had already parlayed some very nice payoffs to the Morgan firm, hadn't he? It was then that I knew that Rick was still smarting from the fallout of the incident at the Annual Dinner. He wanted to prove that he was a valuable asset despite his bad boy ways.

On Friday, the paralegal assigned to the Naples case was told by her supervisor that her travel had not been approved. Rick was livid. The trial was set for the next week and he was relying on a full supporting cast, including the paralegal. By Friday night, efforts to reverse the decision had been fruitless. He appealed directly to John Morgan on Saturday and was told point blank that he needed to clean up and win without the paralegal going. I read their heated e-mail exchanges and prayed that Rick would not only win, but win big. He did.

A week later, the Monday before Thanksgiving, Rick was back in Tallahassee. He came to the office around 11:00 a.m. He was dressed in an ill fitting black jogging suit, white sneakers, and dripping with sweat. His hair was matted and his complexion had a light grey pallor set off against clown red cheeks. Rick always thought he could eat, drink, and do whatever he wanted to his body and all it would take would be a long, exhausting run and all would be cleansed. His poor body was screaming out for good nutrition and rest, but Rick was trying to beat it into submission. The only time he ate well was when I packed extra food for lunch and took some into him on a plate.

David does all the cooking in our home (except Thanksgiving, which is my one day to stay in the kitchen all day and then swear off the experience for another year), and each day is a gourmet's delight. On each feeding occasion Rick would gobble down the entire plate of food I'd given him, groan about his too full stomach afterward, and then warn me, "Jude, when you die I'm going to marry David!" "The line forms to the left," I'd retort. I tried in vain to make him drink water at his desk, but he'd shove it aside and make a joke about only expensive Scotch running through his veins. This day, there would be no gourmet lunch or jokes.

I followed him into his office. He plopped down in his chair and looked up at me with dilated pupils and whined, "Why is John Morgan being so mean to me?" My brain was exploding and the rage was welling up inside of me. I could no longer allow this adult delinquent any more free passes at his and all of our expenses. I leaned across his desk, looked him straight in the eye, and clenching my teeth said, "Do you think I'm stupid?! Look at you! You are an embarrassment. Go home. Call it in! What if a judge or a client came in right now and saw you like this?! Go get it together!" He looked like a balloon with a slow leak. When he finally spoke, he said angrily, "I'm going to take a nap and when I come back, I want the runner to go get the crab claws."

Rick made his refreshed appearance the next day around mid-morning. I dispatched our runner to St. Marks to buy the large cooler full of stone crab claws that Rick enjoyed sharing with his family at the Woodbine Thanksgiving gatherings. He always made sure to treat me to some as well. By 2:00 p.m., his truck was loaded with supplies and crab claws and he was bound for Georgia. He told all of us to take the rest of the week off and that he would see us the following Monday. He really enjoyed the holidays and felt it was important for families to spend as much time together as possible at those special times. This season was an especially poignant occasion for him in that respect. His daughter, Callie, from whom he had been estranged for the past two years, was expecting a baby boy. Rick was heartbroken over not seeing her and knowing that he would have to fight for a chance to see the baby when he arrived.

I was startled to find Rick already behind his desk the next Monday morning around 8:00 a.m. "Where the hell have you been?!" he called out to me in a mocked tone. I laughed and went into his office to ask about his holiday. "It was okay. You know." I told him that once again I had made my threat to not make anymore Thanksgiving meals until I got a new kitchen. David and I are ongoing remodelers at our little house and the kitchen has always seemed to slide down the list of priorities.

As it turned out, Rick had omitted the story of his driving to Winter Park the day after Thanksgiving where he met up with Julie and her husband for dinner. Julie and Rick would be meeting in Orlando with the primary funding source for Southern Communities Foundation after his return from Atlanta in a week, so she was in town now to finalize some due diligence before heading back to Tallahassee. One of her girlfriends was also in town and would join the threesome at dinner. The trip was a spur of the moment one for Rick that ended up changing the lives of a working mother and her children:

*Rick, Chad, and I were meeting a friend of mine, also named Julie, for dinner at the Bohemian Restaurant in Orlando. Rick had brought with him the remainder of the crab claws he bought each year to take to Woodbine for the family Thanksgiving meal. He had them in a small cooler and kept joking that it was his heart in there as he put it on the table. He was in rare form and he and Chad were singing, "Strangers in the Night" to each other. Everyone in the place was laughing and looking at our table as if they were wishing they could join us.*

*Rick insisted on buying our dinners. He threw down some money on the table and we all went outside to wait for our cars to be brought around. Julie's car came first, but before she got into it our waitress came running out of the restaurant, saw Rick and threw her arms around his neck. She was crying and said that God must have sent him because now she could give her children a real Christmas. She said she hadn't known how she was going to give them anything since their dad had left them and they were living from week to week on what she made. And now, Rick was giving her the chance to give them the best one they'd had yet! Rick pulled her off of him and said with a smile, "Well, I think Christmas is a big deal." I don't know how much he had tipped her, but based on the way she reacted, it must have been a lot more than twenty percent!*

*Julie thanked Rick for a good time and drove off. Chad and I got into Rick's car. As we were riding out of the parking lot, he asked me if I thought Julie had liked him. I told him I was sure she did, but explained that she was separated from her husband and was trying to work things out. She didn't want to start anything new until she knew the marriage was really over. He said that was a shame, because he thought she was someone he'd like to know better. One week later, Rick died. A few days after that, Julie called me, full of regret about Rick. She said she had just found out her husband had been having a long term affair.*

Rick and I shared the turkey leftovers I'd brought for lunch in the conference room and then he told me he was going to Orlando early in the morning. "Why? I didn't think you had anything big down there for a couple of weeks. What about our hearing coming up and the interrogatories due on the Leon County lawsuit?" He told me that he planned to work on those remotely, that he had full confidence in our intern on the matters at hand, and that once he lined up some things at Morgan he'd be back in full swing on December 5. His cell phone rang and interrupted our conversation. It was Bridgette calling. I left him to his privacy and went into my office and closed the door. Something was wrong, but I didn't know what it was. The whole atmosphere in the building seemed heavy and thick, like time and energy were suspended.

After the call, Rick stuck his head in my door and displayed a new energy. He had a change in plans. He would be in Tallahassee this week for a couple days more after all. Bridgette was coming to town. She had begun designing some specialty jewelry and she and Rick would be getting together to decide the best way to market it. He was so proud of her and what she was doing. I was grateful that her call had broken the eerie mood I was feeling. Then another thought jolted me. The check to the bankruptcy court! Had he sent it from Orlando?! I jumped up, threw open my door, and yelled out to him, "Rick, did you pay the trustee the money for your stuff?" "What stuff?" "Oh, my God, Rick! You signed a promissory note to pay $25,000 to the court to retain all of your personal things! It was due at least a week ago!" He bolted out of the office and didn't return for an hour. He came back with cash and dumped it on my desk. "Where did that come from?!" I asked incredulously. "It's a loan. We need to draft a letter to go with it. Let's send the runner to Pensacola to hand deliver it now," he demanded. I had heard the rumors of Rick hiding money in various places like boxes buried in his backyard, folded envelopes in cereal boxes, or zippered plastic bags inside toilet tanks. I never came across any of it when we had to stage the Sixth Avenue house for the estate sale, so I can only assume these rumors were urban legend. While I drafted the letter, I had our runner go to the bank and get a cashier's check. When he returned I gave him the letter to go with the check and the directions to the trustee's office in Pensacola.

It's funny how random thoughts can circle around in cyberspace, land in your brain, and then act like magnets to pull positive or negative energy from where they generated. That was what I felt earlier when Rick took the call from Bridgette. The heavy sensation portended a negative power would rain down with vengeance. It had started with the thought of the unpaid promissory note to the bankruptcy court, and then pulled a second assault with it moments later. Just as our runner was driving away, my computer screen flashed an alert of a new filing in Rick's bankruptcy. The trustee had filed an Amended Motion for Turnover. In addition to demanding payment on the promissory note, the motion declared that the trustee had become aware (read – somebody reported a suspicion to the court) that Rick had land holdings in Georgia that he had not declared on his schedules. What this meant was that the entire bankruptcy could be re-opened and lots of misery could follow. I printed out the filing and took it into Rick.

He collapsed back in his chair and looked up at me in bewilderment. "What now?" he asked. "Well, we just took care of the payment, so check that one off. As far as the parcels listed, I'm more than sure that we provided that information as pledged collateral for loans. It will take me a little time, but I'll go through the notebooks we provided to your attorney and see where the information is so he can file an answer on your behalf." Rick was silent and looked defeated. He thanked me and turned his attention to his computer.

It took me most of the next day, but I finally located the Official Record book and page numbers for each filing of assignment, copies of the deeds, copies of the loan

205

documents reflecting the collateral assignment, and e-mails between us and Rick's attorney reflecting some of this from earlier in the year. I bundled it all together and gave it to Rick. It was now after 6:00 p.m., but he told me to e-mail it to his attorney before I left so he'd have it to file in the morning. I turned to leave his office when he stopped me with, "Jude, I don't know how you do it, but you always seem to be able to get my ass out of a sling. You're incredible, and I love you." I smiled and said, "You're welcome."

I sent the e-mail and shut down my computer. Rick was packing up and leaving the office as well. Bridgette would be here tomorrow and Rick had set up an appointment with a patent attorney to meet with them about registering her jewelry designs. I called out "Good night!" to him and hoped that he would find some peace that night and get some needed rest. He was starting to look a little puffy and I was worried that his chronic stomach inflammation issue was bothering him again. He had been in and out of digestive clinics and hospitals for treatment of various ailments in his gastro intestinal tract. Nothing seemed to bring him lasting relief, but the visits did provide additional prescriptions for pain killers, which I feared he used to excess.

As I walked through the reception area toward the front door, that ominous feeling of dread hit me again. I made a mental note to buy some sage to smudge the place on Sunday when I planned to come in and start decorating for Christmas. (Smudging is a Native American practice of burning sage and other dried herbs to purify a room and clear negative energies.) "Nothing like the smell of smudge and cinnamon to put you in a holiday mood!" I said out loud to no one.

Rick called me the next morning to say that he wouldn't be in until after lunch. He and "B" would be going over her designs, meeting with the attorney, and having lunch before coming into the office. "She has a present for you," Rick said with a tease. "Oh, goodie!" I responded. When they arrived, Bridgette came into my office and Rick went into his. As usual, she was lovely - so slender and always dressed in an updated Bohemian style. Her long black hair was tied back in a ponytail and her arms were festooned with beautiful cuff bracelets. She came around my desk and we hugged. She gave me a box containing one of her unique leather and gemstone designs. We chatted for a few minutes about her new business when I noticed that Rick wasn't joining us, which he normally did. I suspected they had either had a fight or some other kind of misunderstanding.

Bridgette got up and went into Rick's office. He called me to come in there as well. "We need to set up an LLC for Bridgette's new company. The name is B-Line Jewelry, Bridgette is Managing Member, use our address, and Bateman Harden is the registered agent." I made the filing electronically and set up the corporation. Shortly thereafter, Rick walked her to her car and then came back inside. We didn't talk about it, but I suspected that he had asked her to go to Atlanta with him that weekend and she declined. I had heard that she was seeing someone pretty seriously over in Seagrove, so that would explain Rick's blue mood.

# Chapter 17

## *The Messengers*

The weather was damp and cold that last Thursday morning of November 2012. I was grateful for it since it put me in the Christmas mood. Decorating a tree in 80 degree weather while wearing a cotton tee shirt and cropped pants was not my idea of a winter wonderland! I looked out my bedroom window and saw that fog was just above ground level. An early start for the office would allow extra driving time in such dicey conditions and I intended to do just that. Rick would be leaving today for Orlando and then on to Atlanta for the weekend, so I wanted to be there when he arrived to go over a few things before he hit the road.

As I approached the turn onto Wakulla Springs Road, I was startled by a flash of something to my right. I stomped on the brakes and looked out the passenger window to see a huge buck deer charging my car! He got within a few feet and stopped, sliding in the gravel on the side of the road. We stared at each other for a moment frozen in time and then he turned and galloped off into the woods. My heart was pounding so hard I could hear the blood rushing in my ears. No other cars were in sight and I was relieved that I hadn't caused an accident from my sudden braking. I drove on and tried to shake off the incident. Within moments, it happened again! This time a deer came racing out of the woods to my left and stopped in the middle of the road in front of me as if it were "playing chicken" with my car. Once again, I stomped the brakes and squealed to a stop within inches of hitting the animal. My fog lights caused a halo effect in the fog around the deer. There was no indication that the animal would move out of the way, so I laid on my horn to give it a startle. That worked, but I was surprised by the nonchalant trot it took to the side of the road rather than an all out sprint. It appeared as if the beast was determining when the encounter would end.

I saw the headlights of another vehicle approaching from my rear, so I quickly drove on. I was flabbergasted by the two incidents. The special deer horns installed on my air intake grill on the front of my car had always worked. In the many years I had been driving this route I had seen countless deer on the sides of roads, but they always reacted to the horns and froze in their steps. They had obviously failed me now and I was going to write the company a long letter about it later in the day. The remainder of my drive into work was uneventful and by the time I unlocked the door to the building I had calmed down, but was ready for some coffee!

An hour later, Rick and Bridgette arrived at the office. I was surprised to see her, thinking she had left the night before. She came into my office and asked me how I was doing. I said, "Well, two deer almost took me out this morning!" and proceeded to tell her the story of my drive into work. Rick was standing in my doorway listening. When I finished the story I looked over at him. His face was ashen and he said in a monotone, "My fondest wish is that I die before you and my children." He walked around my desk and hugged me hard from behind. I was a bit taken aback by his behavior and stood up. I nervously laughed, "Wow! I didn't know I was that important, Mr. Bateman!" With that, he grabbed me again and gave me an even stronger hug. "Someone needs a hug this morning!" I joked as I pulled away. Bridgette had left the room and now Rick was walking out as well. She called out to me that she was leaving and I wished her "Happy Holidays!" from my desk.

Rick and I went over the few case related items I needed from him. I watched him as he read the documents, made some changes, and handed them back to me. His face was puffy and the color of his skin was pale. "Are you feeling unwell?" I inquired. "Yeah, my stomach is bothering me again and I haven't really slept well for days," he confessed. "Why don't you cancel your trip and just stay home and rest?" I pleaded, knowing full well that would be the last thing he would ever do. He ignored me and started throwing some things in his briefcase, so I went upstairs to meet with our paralegal about the documents Rick had just edited.

"I'll see you guys on Monday! Have a great weekend...love you!" he shouted up the stairway. "Rick! Wait a minute, please!" I yelled back. I limped down the stairs and met him in the foyer. "Can you spare just another minute for us to have a chat, please?" "Sure," he said and took a seat in the reception area. I stood in front of him and started, "We've discussed this before, but I really need you to think seriously about it now. My body is a wreck. I have put off surgery for years and the past few months of twelve and fifteen hour days have taken a huge toll on my health." Rick looked up at me and cried, "You're not leaving me, are you?!" "No, Rick. No. I've told you before that I've made a commitment to work with you at least three more years. But, we have to make some changes. I just can't keep up this schedule anymore and I'd like us to come up with an arrangement when you get back from your trip."

He stood up and took my hand. "I've already made some decisions in my own mind. When I get back on Monday, we'll put a plan together. Right now, my goal is to win these three cases coming up and get us around a million and a half in fees. Julie and I are meeting with the funders next Wednesday and soon we can start charging the foundation for legal services to cover our monthly expenses. After that, I plan to tell John Morgan to kiss my ass and you and I will re-start Bateman Harden and have only a few hand picked clients that we want to work with. Most of our time will be working on Southern Communities with Julie. I'll do whatever you need so you can start feeling better." "Sounds good!" I said with a smile. He kissed my hand and walked out the door.

Rick drove to Orlando that Thursday and took care of some business as well as getting together with Laura. They had breakfast together on Friday morning. He had asked her to go with him to the University of Alabama vs. University of Georgia game in Atlanta, but she declined. He then traveled back to Tallahassee and picked up a young lady he had been seeing for a couple of months and headed to Georgia. They arrived at their hotel late Friday afternoon, had an early dinner and retired to their room for the remainder of the evening.

The schedule for the weekend included an early departure for the stadium on Saturday morning, then to meet up with other University of Georgia fans, watch the game through the third quarter, go back to the hotel and party in the hotel bar until the wee small hours of Sunday morning, sleep in late, and return to Tallahassee early Sunday night. The plan changed when Rick complained that he wasn't feeling well and the decision was made to not attend the game. He preferred to stay at the hotel and watch the college football game on television screens mounted in the bar area while throwing back drinks without worrying about driving. By halftime of the championship gridiron battle, he had already decided he wanted to get out of Atlanta earlier than planned. He resolved to meet his good friend, Charlie, for a hunting trip the next day:

> *That last weekend when he was in Atlanta for the SEC Championship game, he called me. He said he didn't feel all that great and probably wouldn't be going to the game that afternoon. He asked when I was shooting doves and I told him the next day. He said that he'd probably leave Atlanta early Sunday morning and would catch up with me to go bird hunting.*
>
> *About noon on Sunday, the birds were flying and he hadn't shown. I kept calling him, but it went right to voice mail, so we went on without him. I got the news the next day that he had died.*

Rick and his date partied until 1:00 a.m. or so and then went back to their room for the night. Around 4:00 a.m., she got up to use the bathroom and heard a gurgling sound coming from him. He was unresponsive to her and she quickly dialed the front desk and asked them to call an ambulance. The paramedics worked on Rick in the room for five minutes without success. They intubated him to hook him up to an oxygen cylinder and raced to Emory University Hospital - Midtown. After the emergency room doctors examined him, he was admitted to the hospital's Intensive Care Unit (ICU) where he was connected to life support machines. His father and brother, Todd, were contacted as next of kin and they quickly drove to the hospital.

Sunday mornings are my lazy times to lie around in my pajamas and enjoy a couple cups of coffee followed by a big breakfast. I was just pouring my second coffee when my cell phone rang around 7:30 a.m. I assumed it was Rick, already breaking his promise to let me have some weekend time without interruption. I looked at the caller identification and saw that it wasn't him after all. It was his friend and business associate, Bill, calling. *Why would he be calling me?* I thought as I took the call and offered a "Good morning!" He mumbled an apology for disturbing my Sunday morning and then proceeded to tell me that Rick was in a hospital in Atlanta and on life support. Instinctively, I knew that he had finally pushed the envelope too far and that big heart had finally given out under the assault of liquor, drugs, and stress. The attack occurred sometime between 1:00 and 4:00 a.m. I asked as many questions as I could, but Bill apologized and said he had very little information himself. He had been called by Todd, since Todd had seen his name and number as one of the last ones dialed on Rick's cell phone. He and his wife were in route to Atlanta while he was calling me. He asked me if I would be driving up. I told him I thought it would better serve Rick if I went to the office instead where I had access to his medical records for the doctors and his Power of Attorney to Bill in case he needed it. The call ended with his promise to call me regularly with updates.

I picked up my purse and ran down the stairs. David was in the yard laying out lines of Christmas lights that he would be draping on our white picket fence after breakfast. I shouted to him that I was going to the office, Rick was in Atlanta on life support, and drove away. Throughout all this time I was in a reactive mode. No emotions, just acting as I knew I needed to. I had driven a few miles when I realized that I needed to contact his cousin, Paul, who he had designated as his Personal Representative in his Will. I called his private cell line and told him about Rick. He asked me to repeat it, since I was talking so fast. I pulled off the road, took a deep breath, and re-told him as much as I knew. I had already Googled the location of the hospital on my cell phone and had that additional information to share. Paul was in Buffalo, New York, on business and said he would get the next plane to Atlanta.

My second call was to Madi, Rick's daughter. No answer. I texted her. She answered by text and told me she knew about her father. By now I had made it to the office and went into my file cabinet to get the "FLB Medical" folder. I'd left my cell phone on my car seat and went out to get it. When I leaned in the passenger side, I saw the red Victorian sled and a white fur clad Santa Claus lying on my back seat. I had put them there the night before as a start to packing up the Christmas decorations I planned to take to the office this day. A tear dripped from my eye. I quickly wiped it away and lectured myself that I had no time for tears just yet. Back in the office, I called the hospital and miraculously got through to the nurse in attendance to Rick. All of those years working with him and watching him charm his way into obtaining information from unsuspecting staffers were paying off!

The nurse confirmed that he was still on life support and that several family members were present. By now, Julie and Chad had also arrived. Rick's date that weekend was an employee of a friend and fellow attorney, and he and his wife had arrived from Tallahassee to take her home. She was devastated and still in shock from the whole experience. I told the nurse that I had all of Rick's medical records and could share them and any other information they needed. She thanked me and asked me to hold. When she came back to the phone she asked me if I could fax the information to her as soon as possible. I warned her it was voluminous, but she said they needed everything to help them determine treatment for Rick. It took 35 minutes for the long transmission to be sent.

By 2:30 p.m., Rick's condition hadn't changed. I called John Morgan's private line and left a voice message. He called me back in five minutes. We chatted briefly and I promised to let him know more as I learned it. My last conversation with Bill was around 5:30 p.m. He told me that the family had decided to wait for the night to pass in hopes that Rick would show some response to treatment. If he didn't, they would make the hard decision of whether or not to allow the machines to continue breathing for him. He also told me that he had used the Power of Attorney I'd e-mailed to him and faxed to the hotel to enter Rick's hotel room and collect his clothing and personal items. He and his wife would spend the night at a hotel and return to the hospital the next morning. I thanked him and we promised to speak again in the morning.

I sat behind Rick's desk and stared out into the reception area. It was getting dark outside and the empty offices made me feel colder. My mouth was dry and when I ran my tongue across my teeth I realized that I hadn't brushed them. I looked down at myself and saw that I was still in my pajamas and slippers. In my race to get to the office I hadn't even changed my clothes, combed my hair, or brushed my teeth. I put my head on my arms and started to moan. Here I was, sitting in the same office that Rick Moore had occupied on that day when he and Karen Bass had told me that Clay wasn't coming back to work. And now, Rick wasn't coming back either. I knew that irreversible damage begins within thirty minutes of blockage of oxygen to the heart muscle. Even if a miracle happened and he came out of his coma, that sapient mind would never be the same. He had been deprived of oxygen for too long and was most likely brain dead at this very moment.

It was now 6:00 p.m. and there was nothing else for me to do. I closed the office and drove home. David had a glass of wine and a light dinner ready for me, but I couldn't swallow anything. A lump had formed in my throat and all I wanted was to awaken from this nightmare. Sleep eluded me that night. I tried to meditate, but thoughts of Rick kept interrupting my attempts. What hadn't I seen? Why didn't I know that he was sicker than he was letting on? Why did I choose the moment before he was leaving to pile on to his heavy emotional load with my demand for more time for myself? Mea culpa! Mea culpa! I was so weary my body felt like it was levitating. I closed my eyes and the deer appeared before me. The deer! That's what they were! They were messengers warning me that something life changing would be happening soon and without warning! Oh, God! Why was I just now putting this together?

I got to the office around 7:00 a.m. on Monday morning. Our interns would not be in the office until the afternoon. Our part-time bookkeeper had been called for jury duty. I had given our paralegal the week off to attend a wedding in New York. The quiet offices really weren't all that different than when Rick was in Orlando. At 9:00 a.m., the phones would start ringing and clients would stop by and that would signal the actual start of the business day. What if someone did stop by this morning? What would I say? My land line rang and interrupted my thoughts of worry. It was Bill. He said that Rick had no change since the night before. The family would be convening at the hospital around 9:30 a.m. to determine what would be done. He said that he would be seeing Rick once more. "Please tell him I ..." I started. I realized that no one could ever communicate what I felt in my heart, so I told Bill it was nothing when he asked me what I had said. I turned on my computer and saw a couple of e-mails from John Morgan. He was inquiring as to Rick's condition. I responded to each and told him that the family would be making a decision soon.

My desk lamp flashed off and on and then my cell phone rang. It was Bill. The family had just given permission for the hospital staff to disconnect Rick from the machine that was performing as an artificial lung to keep oxygen pumping through him. A high pitched beep sounded as the machine shut down, and the heart monitor screen showed only a long, flat line. He was officially pronounced dead at 10:00 a.m. The cause of death was myocardial infarction, commonly known as a heart attack.

After acknowledging to Bill what he had just told me, I turned to my computer and typed a brief e-mail to John. I then crafted another one to go out to clients and friends: "At 10:00 a.m. EST, December 3, 2012, Frederick Leo "Rick" Bateman, Jr. left this earth."

# Chapter 18

## *Celebration of Life*

Within an hour of my e-mail advising of Rick's death, the phone lines were ringing non-stop and my e-mail inbox was exploding with inquiries and messages of condolences. I had already prepared a two line response to recite to anyone who inquired by phone as to what happened, and it proved a wise move. I would not allow myself to feel any emotion at this time. I owed it to Rick to be courteous yet formal with everyone as a sign of respect for his memory. The only time I was close to losing my calm demeanor was when Karen Bass showed up at my door. Of all people. How perfect. She gave me a hug and said how unbelievable it was that I was going through a similar experience that I'd had with Clay's passing. We spoke briefly and she offered whatever assistance I might need.

I needed to reach out to someone in the family to determine what funeral arrangements were being made since I had Rick's written wishes. I called Todd. He was crying and told me that he would call me in the morning to go over things. I thanked him and gave him my deepest regrets. He called me around 1:00 p.m. on Tuesday. He sounded, as expected, completely drained. He said that the family had settled on Thursday for a viewing in Camilla, with a private burial ceremony there on Friday. I asked about Tallahassee. "I understand that's what you want to do for the family in Camilla, but what are you doing about Tallahassee?" Todd told me that the family did not want a ceremony in Tallahassee. "You need to understand, Jude. Rick is ours. We want to bury him with respect. People in other places only think of him as a rowdy, crazy guy who was the subject of some off color jokes." My heart was jumping out of my chest! There was no way Rick couldn't be celebrated in a town that treated him like a rock star! "Todd, please. You need to let me organize something here. There are hundreds of people who want to pay their respects and this is the venue to do that. He made his name here. His homes are here. His children are here. If I promise to put it together and use good taste, no bawdy references, will you let me, please?" He wasn't an easy sell, but after a few more moments of my pledging to handle everything personally, he agreed. The family viewing would still be on Thursday night in Camilla, but the open "Celebration of Life" that Rick had imagined would be on Friday morning in Tallahassee. We would all drive to Camilla afterward for the interment. Now all I had to do was put something wonderful together in forty-eight hours!

In my time, I had written dozens of songs, skits, plays, and parodies, even won some awards along the way. But I never had to put together a funeral production to honor the life of a legend. The phones continued to ring incessantly and clients had begun to stop by to pay their respects and ask about their cases. I was running out of time to get Rick's service lined up! I quickly typed out a rough draft of how I saw the service going from start to end. All that was left was to fill in the cast of players, coordinate the timing of musical accompaniment, casket arrival, family seating, music selections, recordings, etc., etc.! Before I could do anything, I needed the venue. Rick was a Christian, but not a church going one. He was Methodist by faith, so I knew immediately which church I wanted for his service.

Trinity United Methodist Church, in the heart of downtown Tallahassee on Park Avenue, was the only choice that made sense and I quickly dialed the number. It is a Tallahassee landmark with a heritage of old Southern hospitality dating back to 1840. Dominating one city block, the red brick facade meets a striking white semi-circular portico in front, with a cascading stairway beginning at street level and continuing up to the foyer of the two-story high sanctuary connecting to an open plaza surrounded by offices and a day school. A stately white steeple that can be seen above office buildings crowns the structure. I spoke with Tony Fotsch, the Associate Minister, who confirmed the December 7 date was available and that there was seating for 600. I booked it and set an appointment with him for the next morning so I could walk through the facility myself to better gauge how I would choreograph the proceedings. After our phone call, I sent a broadcast e-mail to Rick's contact list advising that a memorial service for Rick would be held on Friday, December 7, 2012, at 11:00 a.m., at Trinity United Methodist Church in Tallahassee.

Next on my list was an officiant. Out of the blue, Bill Proctor's name came to me. Bill was an elected Leon County Commissioner who I knew was also a lay minister. He would be perfect! He, like Rick, courted controversy and always made me laugh when I heard him being interviewed on some hot topic. But, I needed to expedite a conversation with him so I called Vince Long, the County Administrator and dear friend of Rick's. When I told Vince I wanted Bill Proctor to officiate Rick's service, he told me that he believed Commissioner Proctor would be honored if he was available on Friday. Within minutes, I got a phone call from Regina, Commissioner Proctor's assistant, confirming his participation.

My program listed some opening music from an organist, Rev. Proctor's call to worship and some prayers, then the comments of three speakers that Rick wanted (with the substitution of Lee Barrett for John Morgan), and a musical interlude before family members spoke. I had heard the FAMU (Florida Agricultural & Mechanical University) Choir and knew they would be amazing for Rick's service. Unfortunately, the university was on winter break, so no dice. My mind was blank. *Come on, Jude! Think!* At that point, Rick's friend, Bill, walked into my office with Rick's overnight bag and briefcase that he'd retrieved from the hotel room in Atlanta. We hugged and he sat down. I went over the program I'd put together so far and asked him if he knew of a good choir. He did! He told me that Heavens Choir was a group associated with a small rural church and he knew of it because the choir director happened to be someone who did odd jobs for him. Even though I knew nothing of them and had never heard them sing, I trusted Bill and asked him to acquire them for me.

Originally, I was going to leave time on the program for individuals from the audience to say a few words about Rick. But, since the service would be at 11:00 a.m. on a business day, I wanted to hold the entire proceedings to one hour. The interment in Camilla, Georgia would be at 2:00 p.m., so we would be cutting it close as it was. I decided that after the choir sang two gospel numbers, Todd and Madi would be the "clean up" speakers before Rev. Proctor's closing prayer. The service would conclude with "Always on My Mind" played on the church's sound system as everyone filed out.

I was almost ready to have the printed schedule copied, but needed to confirm the arrival of Rick's casket to work that in. I called Todd and went to voice mail. I left a message: "Todd, can you ask the funeral home folks when they expect to arrive in Tallahassee with Rick's casket, please? I need that information to complete the program." He called me back Wednesday morning. "Jude, I don't think they can take the body across state lines. They're only licensed in Georgia," he said in a low tone. *Oh, no! Now what?!* "Okay, Todd. Well, can you tell me the names of the pallbearers you're using for Friday's interment?" He gave me the names and I wrote them down. "If we won't have a casket, I'm going to ask some of Rick's friends from here to serve as pallbearers as well for the purpose of the service program. Is that okay with you?" "Sure." A quick e-mail to four of Rick's closest friends asking them to act as pallbearers, which was answered by everyone immediately, completed my "to do" list. I chose Rick's favorite photo of himself for the front of the program. Our runner delivered the drafted schedule to our contract printer with the direction that I needed the finished product in my hands by 9:00 a.m. the next day!

My phone alarm sounded to tell me it was time for my meeting at the church. I arrived just five minutes late. The sanctuary was even more beautiful than I'd imagined and I knew Rick would be pleased. Tony was gracious and answered the rapid fire questions I shot at him. I told him that I'm a stickler for detail, so to help put my mind at ease, could I hold a dress rehearsal at the church Thursday afternoon. He said there was no problem with that and we shook hands. As I was walking out, he called after me. "Jude, when will the flowers be arriving and how do you want us to set them up?" Flowers?! I had told everyone NOT to send flowers since I knew the family would be receiving lots of them for Thursday's service in Camilla. "Can I get back to you on that, please?" I walked two blocks to the closest florist and quickly ordered several large plants and sprays of flowers for delivery Friday morning to fill in the front of the church. Since there would be no casket, I figured the best substitution would be photos of Rick throughout his life. But, Callie and Madi had already taken most of the photos from the office and from Rick's house on Sixth Avenue. No matter. I'd make do and put whatever I had up front with the flowers.

When I returned to my office, Paul was waiting for me. He wanted to go over the case list and financials since he would be the court appointed executor of Rick's estate. We met with one of our interns and made notes on the case list for action the following week. I told Paul about the memorial service plans and he agreed to be at the church the next day at 3:00 p.m. for the rehearsal and then would go on to Camilla for the family service there. I contacted everyone else who had a role in the program and asked them to come to the dress rehearsal so we could all walk through the show. Yes, I said show. I realized my gaff later and felt embarrassed at first, but eventually laughed it off. Of course, it would be a show! The greatest on earth if Rick was attached to it!

The Thursday dress rehearsal got mixed reviews. It was hard to block the time when one person after another complained that I wasn't giving them enough of it. Lee Barrett couldn't attend since he planned to arrive in town the next day, just in time for the service. Rev. Proctor just nodded when I gave him instruction. The choir director showed up late, and I had to walk through the entrance and exit strategy with him to communicate to the others. He couldn't tell me what songs they would be singing and I cautioned him about needing songs with tempos that would allow the group to sing, clap, and walk at the same time. Tony stopped by with the easels for the photos I planned to place in front of the pulpit area, which I then realized would block the progress of the choir. By 4:00 p.m., all details had been worked out as best as they could be and I said a silent prayer for God's (and Rick's) assistance to make things go well the next day! I handed a CD to Tony containing the Willie Nelson song to be played at the end of the service and he said that he would share it with the church's music director. For insurance, I'd had our runner download the one song to be played through the sound system onto a blank disc so a mistake of selecting the wrong song from a commercial album could be avoided. I shuddered at the thought of another selection, like "Whiskey River", assaulting the serenity of the house of worship!

One more call to Todd and I would end my day. I called him on my cell phone as I was driving away from the church. I needed to let him know about the family lounge downstairs where Rick's parents and other immediate family could convene and receive well wishers. As we spoke, I asked him when the limousines would arrive with the family the next day. He told me that the funeral home only had one limousine, which was a hearse, and it would be occupied by

Rick's casket for transport to the cemetery. "Well, how are your mother and father and the others getting here?" He told me they would all probably just drive their own cars and trucks and meet there. "No! Rick Bateman would haunt me to eternity if I let his father and mother have to fend for themselves that way! Don't worry, I'll make arrangements for a limousine to go to your father's house and as many of you can pile in as you see fit." Todd objected and said that his parents would be uncomfortable with that kind of fuss, but I insisted.

I scrolled through my contacts and found the limousine service that Rick used. When I told them why I was calling, they said that even with the short notice they would try to find a black limo for me and call me back. An hour later, the owner called to apologize for not being able to help. He told me that the one black limo that was the best for the job had some engine trouble and he wouldn't trust it to make the trip between Tallahassee and Camilla twice in the same day. I asked him if he could recommend another service, that I was desperate. He said that he did have one limo available that would not only hold the entire Bateman clan, but was in perfect shape. "Well, why didn't you say so?!" "The problem is that it's white, not black." "Beggars can't be choosers! I'll take it!" "And, it's not a Lincoln." "What is it?" "A Hummer." My mind immediately saw a long, white tricked out military inspired land yacht with elevated flooring that vibrated to Jay-Z rap while bright green, fuzzy dice swung from the rearview mirror. I started giggling. "Ma'am? Did you want me to reserve it for you?" "Of course! It will be great!" I gave him the directions and schedule of events. I ended the call and laughed until I cried. I looked upward and acknowledged the spiritual help that solved my problem. "Thanks, Rick! I know you made that one happen!"

Friday morning was sunny with a cool breeze, just enough to require a sweater or light coat. I arrived at the church a little before 10:00 a.m. and went in the rear entrance so I could check in with Tony before going upstairs to wait for "my program stars" to arrive. He told me the Batemans were already in the family lounge so I went in to greet them. Without exception, each of the large gathering told me how grateful they were for all I was doing and how Rick would be so proud. I was in my stage director mode and tried to deflect the deep emotional current coursing through that room. But, it was easier said than done. After a few minutes, I excused myself and went upstairs to check on the flowers and photo display. People were already arriving and selecting their seats. I walked down the long aisle into the foyer and looked out front. There it was in all of its glory...the huge white Hummer limo with shiny aluminum wheels reflecting rays of the bright sun. Curious pedestrians had to walk around it in order to get to the stairs entering the church. I smiled and knew that it was a sign that the day would be extraordinary.

The audience was a virtual "Who's Who" of politics, business, and entertainment. There were also many former employees of the law firm and workers from Rick's farm and homes. Both of his ex-wives were there as were about 80% of past and present girlfriends. People had traveled from as far away as Canada to be there and honor Rick. I sent word downstairs for the family members to come up so we could get started. As soon as they were seated, I looked at my watch and saw that it was five minutes until 11:00 a.m. I asked the organist to continue playing until Rev. Proctor showed up, but he told me he had contracted for fifteen minutes and the time was up. I thought it best not to spill blood in God's house, so I resisted the urge to strangle him in his seat. I went backstage to ask if anyone had seen Rev. Proctor. No one had. Tony appeared. I told him that I was missing my minister and would be searching the entire property for him. He suggested that he go out and welcome everyone to Trinity to kill some time. I blessed him. I spotted Vince Long in the pallbearers' row and motioned to him to come to me. "Where is Bill Proctor?! I've called his cell phone and Regina's and there is no answer! Do you have a secret number you can use to find him?!" Vince told me he'd try to track him down and stepped outside with his phone.

*Please don't do this! Where are you?!* I was screaming inside as I walked from one doorway to another in the huge building. Suddenly, I heard footsteps on a stairway behind me. Bill Proctor, dressed in his robe and sash, was trudging up the concrete steps with a bewildered look on his face. "There you are!" I said as cheerily as I could muster, given my stressed out state. It turned out that he had been there for thirty minutes. Someone from the church had put him in a waiting area downstairs and hadn't bothered to tell anyone. But, he was just fine. Without missing a beat, he walked out before the assembly and began his message that would move everyone to laughter and tears. The theme of his presentation was his likening Rick to one of Jesus' disciples:

*We have gathered today for a celebration and remembrance of the life of one Frederick Leo 'Rick' Bateman, Jr. This morning catches us by surprise. This is not an activity we had penciled in for this date. But, God in his wise providence saw fit for this day to be one for the community to come together to remember his son, Rick Bateman.*

*It was difficult this week pondering comments for today. We thank God for the powerful life force of Rick Bateman. We have been told to cast no judgment on the lives of others else we shall also be judged. I am honored to serve in the capacity afforded me by this family. In a sense, I am an alter ego of Rick, making me fit for this occasion. This is a celebration of a rare, gifted, complex, courageous, and extraordinary man. I believe beyond a shadow of a doubt that he was a child of God, perhaps a contrarian, but a dutiful son of God. The combined traits of Rick Bateman could more typically be observed in biblical stars. He could have been a great deacon, or steward, or church officer. But many folks would have not liked him. Well, guess what? Church people disliked Jesus, too. And every time Jesus went to the church, he was called out, run out, or he ran others out. He was always questioned about his background, being from Camilla, you know, Nazareth.*

*Never good enough, held in suspect, Jesus was accused of breaking the establishment's rules: healing on the Sabbath, committing blasphemy. There were always problems for Jesus down at the church. He didn't mess with church folk too tough. He just enjoyed life and helping ordinary people. I'm going to go a little bit further today and say that Rick Bateman could have been one of Jesus' twelve disciples. Like several of them, Rick was an avid fisherman, liked the water, likely would have been there when Jesus was passing by. Rick was daring and you all know that he would have beat Peter jumping out of the boat to walk on water to meet Jesus! He would have done that! And the reason I know he would have beaten Peter is because Peter would have had to take off both his shoes and socks. Rick had only to remove his shoes.*

*Jesus had a difficult time with self righteous, holier than thou types and Rick had problems with the same type. No one here today can accurately accuse Rick Bateman of being so heavily focused that he could do no earthly good. Like Jesus, Rick did not let hypocrites interfere with or control him. Eating with tax collectors and holding easy conversation with wine bibbers was not beyond Jesus, nor was it beyond Rick. Rick would eat dinner in public with lowly me! No matter how badly the media had reported on or nailed me to a cross. Rick would not have been troubled at all if Jesus had stopped by a well to speak with a Samaritan woman. Rick, just like Jesus, communicated, interacted, and mingled with all races, period. He did not allow the privilege of his skin to rob him of meaningful association with those whose skin held less privilege in society. There were no lines of demarcation or separation for Rick.*

*Bateman, unlike Peter, did not need a vision on a rooftop. He was just born knowing that God is no respecter of person. Rick took me and my son home with him, invited me often to go fishing. I met his folks in Camilla, Georgia, caught fish out of their lake. They all treated me right. The fact that I'm here before you today in Trinity Church is a powerful reminder and is indicative that the Batemans ain't no respecter of persons. Something good, even in Rick's death, is being said about his mind frame and his attitude of acceptance regardless of one's standing in life.*

*Something special was in my friend. Jesus the Christ attracted the heart and soul of Bateman. He joined the church early in his life and his swagger was grounded in his faith in God and in his own ability. Many people want bible toting and scripture quoting zealots and saints. Well, Rick was not a saint and I'm not either and you ain't neither. But, he had plenty*

*of good works as his legacy, and faith without
works is dead.*

*Although a rare and great lawyer, Rick was
not a prissy. He related to the poor. Rick was no
stuck up, he wanted to give sight to the blind. He
cared for the broken and the bruised...*

I sat down next to my husband and finally let myself
relax. It was going to be alright. Rev. Proctor had captured
the essence of the man and the moment. He set the tone for
the remainder of the service. Paul was next to speak, and
reminisced of the many outings he'd shared with his cousin.
The personal pain he was feeling was palpable. Lee Barrett's
comments followed Paul's and served as the comic relief. He
shared yarns from college days and how Rick would steal his
stories and claim them for his own. He was wonderful. I was
up next. I didn't offer much in the way of my own feelings
and experiences, instead deferring to reading an e-mail from
David Oliver from Morgan & Morgan. He'd only known Rick a
brief time, but he encapsulated the character of the man in
that one missive.

As I walked back to my seat, I nodded the signal for the
choir to burst through the front door and start clapping and
singing as they walked down the aisle to the front of the
church. All heads turned to watch the mix of young and old
singers, dressed in humble street clothes, walk to the beat of
their clapping hands. This was what gospel music was meant
to look and sound like. The assemblage was riveted. The
choir stopped in the front of the church, finished their song,
began another, and then slowly filed back down the aisle,

clapping and singing through the door onto the street: a second of silence, and then an eruption of applause. The audience couldn't help themselves. It was pure and raw, just like Rick.

Todd spoke for the Bateman family. He shared childhood remembrances and how he had always looked up to his big brother - so touching. And then Madi got up to speak on behalf of herself and her sister. The petite blonde with green streaks in her hair spoke softly as she shared cherished stories of their childhood, and how grateful she was to have attended the University of Central Florida in Orlando, where she could spend some quality time with her dad in his last years while he worked there. I could hear the poet in her that left no doubt that she was her father's soul child.

Rev. Proctor closed the service with a prayer and instruction about travel to Camilla. I whispered to David how glad I was that I had asked the church to record the entire service. This was exactly what Rick had envisioned, and for some who couldn't make it, and for those who spoke, I wanted to have a remembrance gift to present to them. Then, Willie's voice came through the sound system and mesmerized the assemblage. It was as if I was hearing the song for the first time and hearing the words coming directly from Rick. I don't know what his intent had been in choosing it. I'm sure some ladies believed it was for them. I believe it was a love song to his daughters. As everyone filed out, I took one last look up front at the display of photos of Rick. He was smiling. "You're welcome," I whispered.

# Epilogue

*"And, in the end, the love you take is equal to
the love you make."*[6]

Rick had said that he wanted to give me something special that last Christmas, and he did. He gave me the gift of time. His death was the end of my professional work life. My schedule was now my own. I spent the first eight months following his demise working with Paul to shut down the law firm, and coordinate an estate sale to liquidate assets to settle up with some of Rick's debtors. I finally scheduled the surgeries I had been putting off and began my journey of self fulfillment. I now have more energy and enjoy more activities than I have in too many years past. I thank him daily for letting me go.

It wasn't until the spring of 2014 that I finally made the decision to write Rick's story. I knew it would take me back to places that I would prefer to forget and stir up some emotional wounds that have yet to heal. I had just finished a book about the feral cats I'd tended to over a period of twenty years at our Spring Creek home, and through whom I had learned so many life lessons. I was ready to move forward with a novel I'd started and then shelved ten years ago. But, phone calls and e-mails from friends and former clients continued to distract me. They told me that they had

---

[6] The Beatles, *"The End,"* Abbey Road album

just thought of Rick and they had to contact me as the closest thing to speaking with him. I knew time was racing by and if I didn't write his book soon, his story would never be told. Rick was one of the few real characters left in the world as I know it, and to deny others the opportunity to meet him through the written word was too sad a thought for me to bear. His friend and former partner, Gary Yordon, said it best: "When we lost Rick, we lost a library...a history library, a government library, a relationship library."

There were times when it felt as if negative forces were working against the project. It would have been easy to just drop the whole effort and go on with my life. I chose to ignore those doubts and claim the book as my own. This is my story of Rick. There were too many blanks I had to fill in on some of his episodes for it to remain a work of nonfiction. I have written it to reflect the man as I knew him. Through our time together, we shared an intimacy that is uncommon and unique. He needed it and I was open to it. Some have said that I knew Rick best. I don't know if that is true. I did know him last, when he was no longer at his zenith and not afraid to show his vulnerability. He had already selected me to write his story, regularly reminding me of my pledge, and telling me to "include that one" whenever a particularly interesting case or incident happened. Maybe that's why he shared so much with me without restriction and gave me such a wide berth in challenging his behavior and confronting him with his shortcomings.

I am indebted to those contributors listed in the front of this book. From the very beginning, they eagerly lined up to share their memories and revel in the time they participated in the "Rick Bateman Experience." To them, I offer my deepest gratitude and affection.

And lastly, I thank Rick for guiding my hand when I had to make hard decisions about some of the tales I needed to tell. His shadow was looking over my shoulder throughout the days and months of writing, and whenever I hit a wall, he pushed me forward. His desire for the truth allayed all my fears. My promise to him is now fulfilled. His soul can be unburdened and I release him to the ether. But, he will remain, "always on my mind."

Made in the USA
Lexington, KY
15 September 2015